IZAPA RELIEF CARVING:

FORM, CONTENT, RULES FOR DESIGN, AND
ROLE IN MESOAMERICAN ART HISTORY AND ARCHAEOLOGY

VIRGINIA G. SMITH

Dumbarton Oaks Research Library and Collection   Washington, D.C. 1984

Library of Congress Cataloging in Publication Data

Smith, Virginia G. (Virginia Grady)
    Izapa relief carving.

    (Studies in pre-Columbian art & archaeology; no.
27)
    Bibliography: p.
    1. Izapa Site (Mexico)   2. Indians of Mexico—
Sculpture.   3. Mayas—Sculpture.   4. Olmecs—Sculpture.
5. Indians of Central America—Sculpture.   I. Title.
II. Series.
E51.S85 no. 27 [F1219.1.C45]   970s [730′.972′75]
ISBN 0–88402–119–X (pbk.)

ACKNOWLEDGMENTS

Special acknowledgment is due to V. Garth Norman for his extensive previous research on Izapa sculpture. All of my drawings of the Izapa stelae and of the motifs from these stelae that I have defined as visual traits are based on photographs published in Norman's *Izapa Sculpture,* Part 1: Album, and Part 2: Text, of the *New World Archaeological Foundation Paper* Number 30.

I also wish to express my gratitude to the late Professor Philip Drucker, who suggested that I make an investigation of Izapa art. My research and the preparation of this paper are in debt to his unfailing encouragement and invaluable guidance.

Contents

List of Figures

List of Tables

Index of Figures Illustrating Izapa Stelae and Related Sculpture

The italicized reference number after each figure corresponds to an illustration of a stela in its entirety; reference numbers in roman are to partial views.

Introduction

IZAPA-STYLE ART consists primarily of the upright stone stelae and associated frog-shaped altars carved in low relief, from the site of Izapa, located near Tapachula, Chiapas, and from certain surrounding sites (Fig. 1). Matthew W. Stirling visited the site in 1941 and described and photographed a number of the monuments (Stirling 1943). Philip Drucker also visited the site briefly in 1947. His test pits by chance revealed only materials from the Postclassic period, including San Juan Plumbate ceramics (Drucker 1948). More recent excavations have been conducted by the New World Archaeological Foundation of Brigham Young University. Beginning in 1962 and extending over four seasons, they have brought the total number of known monuments to eighty-seven upright stone stelae and eighty-nine altars, including both carved and uncarved works (Norman 1973: 1). The site, however, is not well known, and the monuments are undated. In spite of very limited evidence, the generally accepted opinion is that Izapa art was the "connecting link in time and space between the earlier Olmec civilization and the Classic Maya" (M. D. Coe 1962: 100). The purpose of this paper is to report the results of a systematic investigation of this hypothesis and to define precisely, classify, and interpret Izapa sculptures as both works of art and records of material culture.

Because of its geographical placement and the productivity of its environment, the Izapa region was an important overland route for travel between Mexico and Central America during Pre- and Posthispanic times (Lowe and Mason 1965: 197). The site of Izapa is on the wet, hilly piedmont just above the narrow Pacific coastal plain. It is included in the geographic area known as the Soconusco, an important cacao-producing region in Aztec and probably earlier times. Streams carrying rich volcanic soil, such as the Rio Izapa which flows through the site, created, along with the climate, an area with great potential for supporting populations in ancient times (Coe and Flannery 1967: 9, 104). The New World Archaeological Foundation excavations indicate that the site was occupied from 1500 B.C. through the Late Classic period. Susanna Ekholm, who analyzed materials and data excavated by Gareth Lowe from Mound 30a, presents evidence showing that the construction of large pyramids and platforms began in Middle Preclassic times (Ekholm 1969: 4). The carving and placement of stelae and altars around the pyramids is supposed by Ekholm (1969: 4) to have begun during the continued building and enlarging of mounds during the Late Preclassic. Since none of the monuments bears dates, this interpretation remains speculative.

Previous studies of the carved stelae from Izapa are limited in scope or unconcerned with the aesthetic content of the carvings. Although many specialists include stone carvings from other sites in their studies of Izapa art, most consider the art style as a transitional intermediary between Olmec and Maya art styles. To date, the most complete formal and iconographic analyses are Jacinto Quirarte's *Izapan-Style Art* (1973) and Garth Norman's text, *Izapa Sculpture* (1976). Quirarte's studies (1973, 1976) are of the top- and baseline designs of fourteen of the best preserved stelae from Izapa, ten monuments from other sites that he considers possibly Izapa in style, and various framing elements from the stelae. Norman's (1976) detailed analysis of the entire corpus of Izapa carving, and his extensive comparisons with sculptures from other cultures, results in his suggesting relationships between an essentially "Olmecoid" Izapa art and that of the Olmecs at La Venta, the Early Classic Maya, and the Zapotecs at Monte

Alban (Norman 1976: 311). Norman sees these genetic relationships with Izapa as based on the irregular occurrence elsewhere of comparable visual traits or motifs. The origins and meanings of most of these traits have not yet been defined, however, and the absence of dates and the limited stylistic analyses of Izapa art leave unsubstantiated the opinion that this art derives from Olmec and is ancestral to Maya art.

This study is a more systematic approach to understanding the form and content of Izapa stone carving. In an effort to be both quantitatively broad and qualitatively precise, I am using traditional formal and iconographic analysis, guided by statistical techniques. These techniques allow a clearer view of the overall configurations of the complex Izapa art style, and they provide a fairly objective basis for evaluating more subjectively derived interpretations of visual traits and iconographic themes.

The twenty-four best preserved stelae from the site of Izapa are analyzed here to establish a stylistic inventory of visual elements and a set of rules for the use of these elements in the processes of design. These twenty-four stelae were chosen from the twenty-eight originally photographed and published by Norman in 1973. Two stelae, numbers 19 and 20, repeat a single motif and are not suited to the kind of study reported here. Stelae 28 and 69 (Norman 1973), as well as the more recently published Stelae 39, 45, 55, 58, and 59 (Norman 1976), are too badly damaged to yield more than fragmentary data. Miscellaneous monuments (many of which are fragmentary or reused), altars, and four-legged thrones (Norman 1976) are considered, where appropriate, for additional visual reference.

An analysis of visual traits or elements, and of the rules for their use in Izapa sculpture, is necessary to understand clearly the stylistic and iconographic themes of this art syle. Only with such a basis can the Izapa-style stelae then be compared to works from other sites of the Guatemala-Chiapas highlands and Pacific slopes (such as Abaj Takalik, Kaminaljuyu, El Baul, Bilbao, Chiapa de Corzo, and El Jobo) to determine if any or all works from these sites are also Izapa in style. A comparison of Izapa visual forms and organization with those of securely dated works from such sites as Monte Alban and Cerro de las Mesas may yield additional data to test the hypothesized chronological placement of Izapa stelae.

The site of Izapa is described as a ceremonial center (Ekholm 1969: 5) because of its pyramid and platform architecture and the practice of erecting stone stelae and altars. The carvings on the stelae present an organized iconography, which implies that there was a standardization of symbols and that the stelae were generally connected with a religious or socio-religious function. Inasmuch as an art style manifests the society's "ultimate sacred propositions" (Rappaport 1971: 29), the present study attempts to make an essential first step toward understanding Izapa art by analyzing the forms and rules for the processes of design. This analysis might later make it possible to reach logical interpretations about Izapa ritual behavior, attitudes towards the environment, systems of food production, and social and religious organization, including the role of the artist in Izapa society. In short, it is hoped that a close and systematic analysis of the Izapa art style can provide ethnographic data that will contribute to a general understanding of the cultural growth and development of the Chiapas-Guatemala cultural area.

Finally, the method and techniques used to establish a stylistic inventory and set of rules for studying design in Izapa art can serve as a model for archaeologists and art historians in reinterpreting, or interpreting for the first time, the art from the sites in the area. The general and unstandardized labelling of sites as "Izapa," or "Olmec," or "Maya"—labelling that is often based on inadequately defined art styles—has caused much confusion in Mesoamerican archaeology and art history. More precise definitions of the form and content of art styles will remove a major obstacle in the path of future studies of Mesoamerican cultural history.

Literature

Most archaeologists and art historians writing about Izapa-style art compare it to Olmec and Maya art, but many also note the distinctness of Izapa stone sculpture. Izapa sculpture is first described by Matthew Stirling (1941), who published a report in 1943 that contained descriptions and photographs of sixteen stelae, several carved altars and miscellaneous monuments, and a number of shaped stones. Stirling's view is that the Izapa style is unique. Although it bears some similarities to the stone art from the Olmec heartland on the southeastern Mexican coast, and to early Maya art, Izapa, he maintains, is nevertheless a singular style (Stirling 1943: 73). Tatiana Proskouriakoff (1950: 177), however, compares Izapa sculpture to that of the Classic Maya and places it, as well as Stelae 1 and 2 from the site of Abaj Takalik and Stela 1 from the site of El Baul, in the Early Classic period. (Proskouriakoff [1950: 102–153] divides Maya art into Early Classic, or late Cycle 8 and early Cycle 9, and Late Classic, or later Cycle 9 and early Cycle 10 works.) She recognizes the resemblance of Izapa art to that of both La Venta and Monte Alban.

Michael D. Coe (1962: 99–100, 1965: 773–774, 1968: 121) suggests that the Izapa style is Olmec-derived and serves as a "connecting link in time and space between the earlier Olmec civilization and the Classic Maya" (1962: 100). He emphasizes that the Izapa stela and altar complexes, the baroque style, and the calendrics (of El Baul Stela 1 only) are features borrowed by the Maya along with the Izapa long-lipped god who became the Maya long-nosed god. Olmec traits found in Izapa art, in Coe's view (1965: 773–774) are: the U element, the St. Andrew's cross, scrollwork skies or clouds, scenes contained within stylized jaguar mouths, the flame-scroll jaguar brow, and the realistic depiction of well fed human forms. Winged figures, certain types of descending deities from the sky, and long-lipped heads are seen as specifically Izapa. Coe also includes works from Kaminaljuyu and Colomba in Guatemala, and from Tres Zapotes on the Gulf Coast of Mexico, in his survey of the Izapa style. Ignacio Bernal (1969: 172), like Coe, sees Izapa sculpture as related to Olmec and designates it as Chiapas-Guatemala to include the sculpture of El Baul and Abaj Takalik. Bernal feels that the sculpture of this area is an important, but not exclusive, influence on the Maya art style.

Suzanne Miles (1965: 242) compares the Izapa-style stelae with highland ceramic phases, and places the monuments in four chronological and stylistic divisions. These divisions are based on her study of the existence and execution of various motifs, from topline designs to jaguars, knobbed crocodile knees, downward-peering heads, dragon heads, fish, trees, etc. Miles (1965: 237–275) believes that the roles and the attention given the visual motifs are indicators of chronological and stylistic types. In addition, she (1965: 251–252) makes some interpretations of meaning, suggesting, for example, that the canoelike form in the upper left of Izapa Stela 6[1] is an early form of the U element and that the figure on Stela 1 is a fishing god. She (1965: 237–238) discusses the Izapa stelae as part of a stylistically related group particular to the Guatemala-Chiapas highlands and Pacific slopes and sees most of the works as primarily religious in function.

Garth Norman (1973: 1–2) describes Izapa sculptural art as "part of a distinctive style of great importance among the Mesoamerican art traditions" but also agrees with the point of view that it is a link between Classic period civilizations and those of Early and Middle Preclassic Olmec. He sees the Izapa art as an Olmec-derived style and "an important key to understanding the origins of much Classic period iconography" as well as Maya hieroglyphic writing (Norman 1973: 2). In his attempt to describe the whole configuration of Izapa art and to define its iconographic relationships, Norman identifies motifs pertaining to nature and planetary symbolism,

---

[1] The index of figures on page v is a guide to the multiple illustrations of Izapa stelae and related sculpture in the back of the book.

life-cycle themes, and a "monotheistic anthropomorphic deity concept" (1976: 9, 11–85). Some motifs, such as profile deity masks, are proposed "barometers" for tracing Izapa stylistic origins and extensions (1976: 311). Overall, Norman views Izapa art as narrative picture writing. He concludes that the designs "functioned essentially as records carved in stone, perhaps as much documentary as were the known Maya or Mixtec codices to which they are antecedent" (1976: 323).

Jacinto Quirarte (1973: 32–33) makes a fairly complete formal and iconographic study of the stelae's top- and baseline designs and narrative frames. Including additional analyses of other visual elements, he proposes groupings of the works that are both chronological and thematic (1973: 26–30, 34). Quirarte reports that while Izapa art is influenced by Olmec cultural ideas and concepts, it is also highly original; as an example, he cites the absence of an Olmec or Maya equivalent for Izapa confrontation scenes involving serpents. Other Izapa traits are: sophisticated use of overlapping, diminution of size, placement of figures to establish a legible spatial framework, abstraction of the open mouth of the feline serpent as a pictorial frame, and use of top- and baseline designs as place indicators (1973: 32–33). Quirarte (1976: 79–85) further discusses double-headed compound creatures and winged figures, terrestrial long-lipped heads, bifurcated tongues, and T-shaped elements to show how the "Olmecs, Izapans, and Maya participated in related traditions, each arriving at different formal and thematic solutions to basically similar world views." He reports the frequency of relationship of visual elements to a feline bearing serpentine and/or saurian attributes. Quirarte (1973: 35) includes in his study of Izapa sculpture, stelae and other carvings from Alvarado, Abaj Takalik, El Baul, El Jobo, Chiapa de Corzo, Kaminaljuyu, La Venta, Tepatlaxco, and Tres Zapotes.

Finally, Mino Badner (1972: 3) traces possible exotic components of the Izapa-style art to Andean artistic influence. He feels that "any serious doubt of connection between Chavin and Izapan art should be dispelled by the strength of the visual and iconographic similarities" that he believes the two styles share (1972: 23). Among these shared characteristics are the double-headed serpent-monster, the entwined or knotted serpent, and the grotesque masked bird-man with extended wings.

Chronology

The Izapa art style's placement in time is variously interpreted (see Fig. 2). Quirarte (1973: 34), for example, reports that the works all fall within the Late Preclassic and Protoclassic periods, ranging from 500 B.C. to c. A.D. 36, the date of El Baul Stela 1. He points out that the geographical position of Izapa, and the dates assigned to the sculpture from Izapa and related sites, make the intermediary role of the Izapa style appropriate and correct (1973: 5). Miles (1965: 273) places the stelae somewhere before 400 B.C. to A.D. 1, and Norman (1973: 1) sees the works as Late Preclassic and Protoclassic. Proskouriakoff (1950: 177) finds only very Early Classic comparisons of Izapa with Maya art styles, while M. D. Coe (1962: 15) suggests a Late Formative (Late Preclassic) placement between 300 B.C. and A.D. 100. Parsons (1969: inside back cover) limits the Izapa stelae to the Protoclassic, which he dates 100 B.C. to A.D. 100. Bernal (1969: 127) associates the stelae with Olmec III, 600 to 100 B.C., or just afterwards in the Late Preclassic, 500 to 100 B.C.

While the geographical location of Izapa is perhaps a strong point in the argument for the art style as a chronological and stylistic intermediary between the Olmec and Maya styles, there are reasons to question this hypothesis. First, the site was occupied, more or less continuously, for about 2500 years, from c. 1500 B.C. through the Postclassic period (Ekholm 1969: 1, 19). One of the earliest examples of mound construction at the site is Mound 30a which represents successive construction periods from the early Middle Preclassic to the Late Preclassic. While Ekholm is probably correct in assigning the earliest mound-building activities at the site to around 700–600 B.C., the practice continued into the Early Classic and was again renewed in the Late Classic.

Despite Ekholm's (1969: 4) assigning the original placement of the Izapa monuments to the Late Preclassic, an assignment based on the tremendous building activity that occurred then, there is actually no way to determine the precise time of the original placement of the monuments. The monuments do not bear dates. Also, as Proskouriakoff suggests (1950: 177), early traits may be retained and thoroughly integrated with later developments and do not necessarily indicate antiquity; thus, stylistic comparisons may be misleading indicators of chronology. Further, while comparisons of Izapa stelae with those of nearby sites such as El Baul, Bilbao, Abaj Takalik, and Kaminaljuyu are of some benefit, it may be misleading for chronological purposes to consider all of these sculptures as a single, interrelated art style. Close examination may reveal that the Izapa art style is distinct not only by comparison with the art of the Classic Maya, but distinct from nearby sites as well.

In general, it is difficult to argue that Izapa should be selected as the particular stylistic or chronological descendant of the earlier Olmec culture. Olmec influences were equally available to other sites and were widespread during Early Formative times when long-distance Pan-Mesoamerican trade routes were well established (Pires-Ferreira 1967b: 313). Then, during the period of regionalization that followed in Middle Formative or Middle Preclassic times, long-distance exchange was reduced as was the potential influence of the center of the Olmec heartland, La Venta (Pires-Ferreira 1967a: 304). Other powerful centers, such as expanding Monte Alban in Oaxaca, would have been more viable sources of information and artistic stimulation for the Izapa elite.

Art and Anthropology

The limitations of studies of non-Western art by anthropologists are due largely to the definition of aesthetic anthropology—the application of anthropological method to aesthetic phenomena. For instance, when Fischer (1961: 81) proposes that "symmetrical design should characterize the egalitarian societies; asymmetrical design should characterize the hierarchical societies," his real interest is social organization, not formal artistic analysis. Some studies of art forms, for example Hatcher's (1967) analysis of Navajo art, rely on basic elements of art historical analysis—color, perspective, or composition—but are so based on psychology as to overshadow art historical interpretation. Other studies identify significant, repeated motifs without pretending to analyze artistic content via underlying form. Drucker's writing on Olmec art (1952) is an example of this kind of straightforward description. Similarly, Miles (1965) selects particular visual traits from art of the Guatemala-Chiapas Pacific Coast sites. Although she is thorough in reporting the various occurrences of these traits, her study is based on a comparison with ceramic phases and does not take into account many basic artistic devices that are present in the art. On the other end of the scale, artist Covarrubias (1946) contributes to an understanding of Olmec art through his drawings of motifs—but personal sensibility, not fundamental aesthetic principles, is the foundation of his interpretation.

Where the anthropologist looks at art as something that helps him investigate, the art historian is interested in works of art as something to be investigated. Both approaches are valuable in cultural historical studies, but to understand how a particular art style reveals, or is a part of, a culture, one must first define that style.

The art historical approach provides a sound body of data from which anthropologists may draw support. A work of art is a cultural-historical document; as the artist's conceptions are largely determined by history and culture, art is bound to reflect the time, place, and society in which it is produced. For this reason, studies of art, especially where written texts do not exist, provide important clues to understanding the culture. On the other hand, one cannot fully analyze or understand art without another important aspect of art history that involves identifying and explaining main characteristics of individual works and the nature of relationships among groups of works (Kleinbauer 1971: 35). When presented with a series of carved stone stelae, the logical beginning of an analysis must lie in the fundamental definitions and procedures of art history rather than hypothesized social organization or religious practice. Indeed, iconography includes description and classification of themes, attitudes, motifs, and the identification of meaning in works of art; iconographic studies must, therefore, be based on careful visual analysis.

Often studies that are primarily art historical contribute simultaneously to the art history and anthropology of non-Western art. For example, Bill Holm's (1965) *Northwest Coast Indian Art* specifically describes this style and its subjects, materials, and techniques of manufacture. His identification of the formline as a characteristic swelling and diminishing linelike figure that delineates design units is useful to all students of Northwest Coast art (1965: 29). Holm's predecessor in these studies, anthropologist Franz Boas, first examined this art in terms of the art itself, addressing such artistic problems as realism and conventionalization.

In Mesoamerican art, Proskouriakoff's publication (1950) is one of the most complete studies to date of variations in the Classic Maya art style. Proskouriakoff finds that aesthetic values and artistic qualities are prerequisites of her research, and writes that "the more comprehensive and more sensitive changes . . . lie in the artist's approach to his subject, in the direction of his attention, and in the stress he imparted to that which interested him in the design" (1950: 2–3). Another contribution to the understanding of Prehispanic Mesoamerican art is Arthur G. Miller's (1973) study of Teotihuacan mural painting, in which he relies on such art historical concerns as composition, image, and color characteristics such as hue, intensity, and value to describe the painting style. Regarding Izapa art, Quirarte (1973, 1976, 1981) is a forerunner with his formal and iconographic analysis of top- and baseline designs along with certain other motifs. A number of his conclusions will be referred to in greater detail throughout this paper.

Art historians Erwin Panofsky and George Kubler offer guides to the research reported here, as both investigate the iconography, or meaning, of art forms through a visual approach that is applicable to arts other than those of Western Europe. Both scholars use art historical procedures that are sufficiently broad based to be significant regardless of the artwork's time, place, or technique of production.

Panofsky (1939: 3–17) outlines the tasks of the iconographer. Similar to, and based on, formal analysis is the identification of natural meanings—or persons, objects, and motifs that are represented by artistic form—that must be recognized from configurations of lines, volumes, and color. The natural meanings identified, the iconographer may move to the discovery of conventional meanings of forms; thus a building is a martyrium, a flower is a lily. Conventional meanings may be ascertained by consulting textual sources and/or traditional artistic representations of the same persons, objects, and motifs. This second level of interpretation is iconography. These two levels of interpretation are presented in this paper. First, close visual analysis defines meaningful forms and motifs. Second, by their context and repeated representation (lacking textual references), meanings of these forms and motifs are identified. Panofsky proposes a third level of interpretation, iconology, which is beyond the scope of this study. Iconologists deal with a work of art as a symptom of the world view at the time at which the work was produced, or as a document of the essential attitudes of the human mind.

Kubler's studies are also useful in this research and in other studies of non-Western art as they help to define an art style by taking into account complex stylistic diffusion, invention, and modification. One of Kubler's aims is to connect art history with the history of material culture (1962: 12–16). As a fundamental concept, he sees all material worked by human hands as series of solutions to various problems. "Linked solutions," or series, are disclosed as "formal sequences" in time (1962: 33). Several formal sequences may coexist within such a complex thing as a Gothic cathedral. Indeed, "everything is a complex having not only traits, each with a different systematic age, but having also clusters of traits, or aspects, each with its own age. . ." (1962: 99).

Kubler applies the idea of iconographic clusters in his work on *The Iconography of the Art of Teotihuacan* and demonstrates that "the entire iconographic system . . . resolves into five or more major clusters of motifs" (1967: 6). He warns those who would study non-Western iconography of "disjunctive situations where form and meaning separate and rejoin in different combinations" (1967: 11) and tells us to beware of the dangers of assuming that similar forms in different times and places must carry similar meanings. Referring to Panofsky (1960: 84) who first cited this "law of disjunction," Kubler further proposes that content may survive in new forms, while older forms may survive with their original meaning replaced by a new content. ("Content" here is used as being nearly synonymous with meaning.) For instance, by examining the context of the feathered serpent's form, we can see that this form has different meanings in different situations. Within the liturgical framework of its iconography, Teotihuacan art shares meanings, but few forms, with Early Classic Maya art at Tikal and Kaminaljuyu (1967: 12–13). Panofsky's (1939) method of arriving at the iconography of an art style through formal analysis, description, contextual classification, and interpretation as well as Kubler's (1962, 1967) elaboration of this approach and his view that the history of formal inventions can be seen in the context of other visual traits and groups of traits, provide a sound method for defining and understanding any art style.

In addition to utilizing general art historical and anthropological methods, my study is designed to approach artistic materials from Izapa through the concepts proposed by Kubler and Panofsky. Initially, an attempt is made to determine formal sequences among the complex of Izapa carved stelae. Aspects of Izapa art, including elements and motifs borrowed from contemporary or previous cultures, can be identified as visual traits and as clusters of visual traits. Izapa formal and iconographic inventions can thus be viewed in the context of a well-defined Izapa art style. Changes that may occur in the meanings of particular forms can also be better recognized by understanding their context in a complex of formal elements.

This study of Izapa stelae proceeds through three essential steps: description, classification, and interpretation. Subdivisions within a step are noted in the sequence in which they are carried out. Description entails isolating the visual traits to be analyzed; classification is the result of determining the rules for the use of these traits in the processes of design. From analysis of the visual elements or traits described in the context of the rules for their use, interpretations of meaning can then be made. In order to move from description to interpretation, a stylistic inventory of Izapa visual traits, and a set of rules for the use of these traits, must first be established.

In preparation for analysis, some basic assumptions must be stated. First, it is assumed that the carvings on Izapa stelae are not the result of haphazard invention or arrangement of forms but are specific visual traits arranged in a systematic manner. It is further assumed that identification of specifically Izapa visual traits and of specifically Izapa rules for the use of these traits will lead to a reliable definition of Izapa-style art. The results of this analysis should yield data for comparison with other stylistically related art styles.

The absence of informants makes it impossible to isolate those elements of design that had a specific cultural meaning or to determine what those meanings were. Reliance is therefore placed on the frequency with which visually meaningful traits occur. To insure that consideration is given only to those visual traits that are a viable part of the Izapa stylistic inventory, only those that appear on at least two different stelae are used. Without such a multiple occurrence, a supposed visual trait might in fact be an unconventional piece of carving.

A further assumption is that a decorative system can exist independently of the specific artifacts to which it is applied. The design elements on Izapa stone carving were not necessarily applied only to stelae but could have been used on textiles, woodcarving, and ceramics as well. It is also assumed that a rule by which any particular arrangement of visual traits is produced can be isolated and stated as a formula. Although any rule given in this analysis is not necessarily the same rule the Izapa sculptors applied when carving the stelae, the rule given here will produce the same result. Even if the visual traits identified here were not seen as distinct by an Izapa artist, repetition of the arbitrarily isolated units produces the same pattern.

Finally, it is assumed that an art form with a standardized set of visual forms and a set of rules for their organization can potentially provide information on aspects of the social and religious beliefs of the culture that produced that art. Reasoning from this, the patterns produced by the organization of visual material can be a source of ethnographic data.

Description

Selection and Definition of Visual Traits

For the purposes of this study, visual traits are specific, complete images. Although these images have component elements of design, they are distinct representations separable from their context. As a major goal of this research is to establish rules for a visual grammar in Izapa-style art, traits are selected only from stelae at Izapa. Stelae from other sites cannot be considered Izapa in style until they are shown to have the same visual traits and the same rules for the use of these traits in the processes of design.

The visual traits analyzed in this study are selected from Izapa Stelae 1–12, 14, 18, 21–27, 50, 60, and 67[2] because these stones are the most complete (see page iv to locate illustrations of the stelae). Further, the carving on most of the stelae is confined to an area framed by top- and baseline designs. However, Stela 27 is divided

into three zones, with carving above and below these designs, and Stela 1 is carved above the topline design. In the interest of uniformity of format, designs outside the top- and baseline frame are excluded. The visual traits are divided into nine groups: 1) Figure-Pose, 2) Ground, 3) Action, 4) Animals, 5) Heads, 6) Glyphs, 7) Objects, 8) Jewelry, and 9) Clothing.

Group I: Figure-Pose. Figure-poses are conventions of the forms by which principal figures are expressed. These conventions can be recognized in any representational art (Arnheim 1954: 74–76). The representation of the figure (whether human or anthropomorphic) and the pose in which it appears are important because they tell the viewer which artistic methods were preferred to represent particular characteristics of the subject. For example, a frontal view can be used to display information about various types of dress and ornament but cannot easily include bustles or trailers on the headdress.

The code, a description of the figure-poses, and the stelae upon which they appear are:

---

[2]These stelae are published in V. Garth Norman's *Izapa Sculpture* (1973: Pls. 1, 3, 5, 7, 9, 11, 13, 15, 17, 19, 21, 23, 25, 27, 33, 35, 37, 39, 41, 43, 45, 49, and 53).

Code	Description	Izapa stelae and figures in the text
FSTAN	standing figure	1 (Fig. 6a), 2 (Fig. 6d), 3 (Fig. 3b), 4 (Fig. 3a), 5 (Fig. 6b, c), 7 (Fig. 7b), 9 (Fig. 5a), 10 (Fig. 4c), 11 (Fig. 16a), 21 (Fig. 4a), 22 (Fig. 8a), 24 (Fig. 54c) (only feet visible), 25 (Fig. 8c), 26 (not illustrated), 27 (Fig. 4b), 50 (Fig. 5b), 60 (Fig. 7a), 67 (Fig. 8b).
FPRST	seated opposing individual figures	5 (Fig. 17b, c), 12 (Fig. 17f), 14 (Fig. 17e), 18 (Fig. 17a), 24 (Fig. 17d).
FSTIN	seated or reclining individual figure	5 (Fig. 9c, d), 6 (Fig. 11), 7 (Fig. 7b), 8 (Fig. 12b), 10 (Fig. 12c), 11 (Fig. 12a), 21 (Fig. 13a), 22 (Fig. 9b), 24 (Fig. 10b), 27 (Fig. 27c), 50 (Fig. 10a), 60 (Fig. 7a), 67 (Fig. 9a).

FFODV	figure falling or diving	2 (Fig. 14a), 4 (Fig. 15b), 23 (Fig. 15a), 27 (Fig. 14b).
FPROF	figure posed in profile or three-quarter view	1 (Fig. 6a), 2 (Fig. 6d), 5 (Fig. 6b, c), 6 (Fig. 11), 7 (Fig. 7b), 8 (Fig. 12b), 9 (Fig. 5a), 10 (Fig. 12c), 12 (Fig. 22b), 14 (Fig. 27a), 18 (Fig. 17a), 22 (Fig. 8a), 23 (Fig. 15a), 24 (Fig. 10b), 25 (Figs. 8c, 13b), 26 (not illustrated), 27 (Fig. 7c), 50 (Fig. 10a), 60 (Fig. 7a), 67 (Fig. 8b).
FFRRP	fractional representation of figure	2 (Fig. 14a), 3 (Fig. 3b), 4 (Fig. 3a), 9 (Fig. 5a "child"), 10 (Fig. 4c), 11 (Figs. 12a, 16a), 21 (Fig. 4a), 22 (Fig. 9b), 27 (Fig. 4b), 50 (Fig. 5b), 60 (Fig. 14c), 67 (Fig. 9a).
FLARG	large figure	1 (Fig. 6a), 2 (Fig. 14a), 3 (Fig. 3b), 4 (Fig. 3a), 5 (Fig. 6c), 6 (Fig. 11), 7 (Fig. 7b), 8 (Fig. 33a), 9 (Fig. 5a), 10 (Fig. 12c), 11 (Figs. 12a, 16a), 12 (Fig. 22b), 14 (Fig. 27a), 18 (Fig. 17a), 21 (Fig. 4a), 22 (Fig. 9b), 23 (Fig. 15a), 24 (not illustrated), 27 (Fig. 7c), 50 (Fig. 10a), 60 (Figs. 7a, 14c), 67 (Fig. 9a).
FSMAL	small figure	2 (Fig. 6d), 5 (Figs. 6c, 17b), 8 (Fig. 12b), 9 (Fig. 5a), 10 (Fig. 4c), 12 (Fig. 17f), 14 (Fig. 17e), 18 (Fig. 17a), 21 (Fig. 27b), 22 (Fig. 8a), 24 (Figs. 10b, 17d), 27 (Fig. 4b), 67 (Fig. 8b).

There is at least one standing figure (FSTAN) on all the stelae except Stelae 6, 12, 14, 18, and 23. As might be expected, a single standing figure is often a large figure (FLARG). A figure is designated as large if it occupies at least two-thirds of the horizontal or one-third of the vertical picture space between top- and baseline designs. A single, dominant, standing figure is shown on Stelae 1, 3, 4, 9, and 24. On Stela 21 there are two large figures, but the figure standing and holding a victim's head is clearly emphasized. On Stela 11 the upper, winged figure is standing behind or in the mouth of a large, crouching, reptilian figure; these two figures are

nearly equal in size. Large figures are also shown seated or reclining (FSTIN) on Stelae 6, 8, 10, 11, 21, 22, 50, 60, and 67, and as falling or diving (FFODV) on Stelae 2, 4, and 23. The small diving figure on Stela 27 is enclosed by a cartouche.

Small figures (FSMAL) are those occupying less than one-third of the vertical or two-thirds of the horizontal picture space and are sometimes shown standing, as on Stelae 2, 5, 10, 21, 22, and 67. They may also be seated as they appear on Stelae 5, 8, 12, 14, 18, 24, and 27. Some seated figures are arranged in opposing pairs (FPRST) near the base of the stela. These figures attend incense burners on Stela 18, the lower left of Stela 5, and the lower right of Stela 24, or fire, as on Stela 12. The pair of seated figures on Stela 14 might have had an incense burner between them; what remains visible of their leaning, cross-legged pose and reaching gestures is similar, if not identical to, the figures attending incense burners on Stela 24. Stela 5 includes another pair of seated figures who gesture over a small *incensario*.

There are a number of fractionally represented figures (FFRRP). They include the standing figures on Stelae 3, 4, 10, 11, 21, and 50; the smaller figure on Stela 27; the small figure being carried on Stela 9; and the seated or reclining figures on Stelae 11, 21, 22, and 67. There is no emphasis on a three-dimensional reality for these figures because they are compressed by representing the head and legs in profile and the trunk and arms frontally. This pose is formal and permits preservation of the symmetry of the chest and shoulders. By matching the natural symmetry of the figure with symmetry in representation, the perceptual impact of the shape is strengthened (Arnheim 1954: 76). This formal pose symbolizes an idea of action rather than representing one phase of a complex action; it might be considered a verb and a principal form in Kubler's (1967: 5) linguistic model of systematic relationships in an art style. Because of its symbolism, it can convey meaning efficiently in terms of number of images. As an indication of the formality of the pose, all of the fractionally represented figures are oriented from the viewer's right to left. Each figure faces his right and has the right foot forward. When one arm is raised above the head, it is always the left arm. One exception in the direction of the gaze may be the head of the falling figure on Stela 4. It appears to be completely drawn back in the manner of the downward-peering heads (cf. Group V).

The rest of the figures—those standing on Stelae 1, 2, 5, 9, 25, 27, and 60, and falling on Stela 23—are shown in profile or three-quarter view (FPROF). The small figure standing on the right side of Stela 22 and possibly (by comparison) the small figure on the corresponding part of

Stela 67 are also described in three-quarter view. In addition, the figures on Stelae 7 and 60 may be interpreted as represented in profile. This pose is suggested by the shoulders of the seated or reclining figure on Stela 7 and the standing figure on Stela 60, and by the similarity of the poses of these two figures. Finally, the swastikalike pose of the upside-down figure on Stela 23 is close to that of the standing figure on Stela 50 with its running legs and bent elbows. Nevertheless, the falling figure is viewed as a profile on the basis of the slight overlapping to show more of the near shoulder and arm. As with the truly fractionally represented figures, the pose is symbolic of action but its modification makes it appear more energetic and expressive. The profile or three-quarter view figure-poses present a more informal, varied, and expressive representation of the figure. These figures are shown three-dimensionally with torsos turned in roughly anatomical agreement with the head and lower body; there is much more variety and expression in their gestures. Also, while the profile figures may function as verbs in Kubler's (1967: 6) model, they are often accessory rather than principal forms. These figures face left or right but always have the inside leg advanced. They are actually performing a phase of a complex movement. In general, the figures shown in profile are posed as they must be to perform an act, while the fractionally represented figures are representative of an action.

Group II: Ground. Ground refers to the imaginary spatial world within the frame of the decorated surface and the visually created distance between the images. Some of the artistic conventions that make spatial illusions are dimunution or size differentiation of the figures, relative placement of the forms in the visual field, and overlapping of forms. These devices are usually not considered by anthropologists, but are primary considerations in art historical analysis (Arnheim 1954: 177–244). When Kubler (1967: 7) discusses the rank of differently posed figures, he is referring, as evidence, to several spatial characteristics. Of those specialists who have written about Izapa art, only Quirarte (1973) considers spatial qualities.

An illusion of depth is used to bring more important subjects to the foreground, or to display simultaneous events that occur at different levels in the picture plane. The visual relationship between viewer and picture ground plane may also indicate differences of time. One example occurs in a continuous narrative when it is understood by the viewer that events shown further away are related but consecutive. The picure plane may be read as receding, or as a continuation of the actual space in which the viewer stands (SRECS). More often, spatial depth is quite shallow (SPLAN). Stela 18 shows a shallow, stagelike use of picture space where overlapping (SOVER) and diminution of size are the conventions. Depth is frequently suggested by vertical perspective (SVERT) when images progressively higher in the picture plane are fur-

ther from the viewer as in Stela 21, or when there is no groundline upon which figures stand, as in Stela 6. A groundline sometimes takes the form of top- and baseline designs in Izapa carvings (SABBL). In this instance the picture plane is divided into upper and lower regions. The visual surface is considered as receding (SRECS) where smaller figures are enclosed in cartouches, although these cartouches may actually represent applications to the surface of other objects (see Stelae 8, 14, 27). While it might more appropriately be labelled "composition" (pertaining to the ordering and arranging of images and shapes within the spatial format of the stelae), a symmetrical arrangement of figures is included as a characteristic of Izapa use of the picture surface (SSYMT). Symmetrical compositions are especially useful to visual organization by uniting a complex series of designs through balance, giving the viewer a central, visual, resting place.

The six basically different uses of ground or picture plane are:

Code	Description	Izapa stelae and figures in the text
SPLAN	shallow spatial depth	1, 2, 3, 4, 5, 6, 7, 8, 10, 11, 12, 18, 21, 22, 24, 27, 50, 60, 67 (Fig. 18a).
SOVER	overlapping of figures	2, 3, 5, 8, 10, 11, 12, 18, 21, 22, 25, 50, 60, 67 (Fig. 18b).
SABBL	picture plane is divided into two regions vertically, as figures stand on, or emerge from, top- and baseline designs	2, 4, 12, (Fig. 19a).
SVERT	vertical perspective, where further images are higher in the picture plane or where figures do not stand on a groundline	2, 5, 6, 7, 9, 21, 22, 24, 25, 50, 60, 67 (Fig. 19b).
SRECS	recessional depth, a carved extension of the actual space in which the viewer stands	8, 14, 27 (Fig. 20a).
SSYMT	if one figure, central placement and bilateral symmetry, if two or more figures, equal placement from the center	2, 4, 5, 8, 9, 11, 12, 14, 18, 22, 23, 67 (Fig. 20b).

Group III: Action. Action is the sum of the relationships between the gestures of the figures and the objects. Certainly, "Motion is the strongest visual appeal to attention" (Arnheim 1954: 304), and the dramatic actions of the Izapa carvings are one of their strongest visual qualities. In Kubler's model (1967: 6) these actions are pictorial verbs. The actions chosen as visual traits are an attempt to type the themes of the stelae, each of which depicts at least one event.[3] Types

of actions are identified by the overall expression of the gestures and postures. For instance, each of the standing figures on Stelae 3, 4, and 21 holds a weapon in the left hand which is raised as if to strike someone or something. Although an actual opponent is not shown on Stela 4, this action has been called "beheading" (DBEHD) because of the human decapitation on Stela 21 and the serpent decapitation on Stela 3. Also, Stela 67 has been coded as showing the holding or wrestling of a "serpent" (DWRST) by reason of the similarity of the scene to Stela 22; additionally, a serpent form winds upward and around the small figure on the central right area of the stela.

Actions shown are:

[3]Norman (1976: 16–17) approaches Izapa themes in a somewhat different manner. Symbolic motifs are combined to express "functional concepts." He stresses the art's complex subjects as symbolic of deities and/or concepts rather than as a more immediate expression of religious activities or actual events.

Code	Description	Izapa stelae and figures in the text
DBEHD	beheading, or posing as if to behead someone	3 (Fig. 3b), 4 (Fig. 3a), 21 (Fig. 4a).
DWRST	holding or wrestling a "serpent"	22 (Figs. 8a, 9b), 50 (Fig. 5b), 67? (Figs. 8b, 9a).
DCHLD	carrying a small person or child on the back	5 (Fig. 6c), 9 (Fig. 5a).
DMOTH	holding something in the mouth or on the tongue	3 (Fig. 21a), 6 (Fig. 21c), 11 (Fig. 21b).

Group IV: Animals or Animal Characteristics. The visual traits listed as animals refer to real or imaginary, part or whole creatures. In some cases outstanding attributes, such as crocodile feet (ACRFT), were chosen to identify the creature. Such attributes would function as adjectives in Kubler's (1967: 6) model. Animals and anthropomorphic or compound (Kubler 1967: 7) creatures are important to understand the meaning of a scene. If these stone carvings are indeed religious in nature, and if the main figures are deities or persons dressed as deities, their domain is more easily identified by their associated environment in nature. For example, if crocodile feet or fins (AFINS) are present for a particular figure, that figure is associated with water. Saurian characteristics are described by Quirarte (1976: 84), who relates them to many themes

of Izapa art. He also (as well as Norman 1973: Pls. 13, 21, 23, 37) points out the use of the double-headed sky serpents (ASSER) and earth serpents (AESER) as pictorial frames. The sky and earth serpents are designated according to placement within the composition. Two-headed serpents that frame the top of a scene are considered sky serpents; those that frame the bottom (and also help define or create a groundline) are earth serpents.

Fish (AFISH) are among the most clearly preserved images on the stelae. They are described as "ring-tailed" by Miles (1965: 241). Three styles of fish are actually identifiable, including what appears to be a kind of crustacean-fish found only on Stela 1 in the basket being lifted from the water. It is included here because of its comparison to the Cerro de las Mesas jade plaque (proba-

13

bly Lower II Horizon, or 600 B.C.) (Berger et al. 1967: 13), described by Drucker as fishlike but with a head that may be "almost any stylized reptile or monster" (Drucker 1955: 46–47), and because of its overall contribution to the theme of water on Stela 1. Further, although the fins are preposterous, this fish might be imagined to represent a gar, presumably *Lepisosteus tropicus,* snapping its jaws (W. I. Follett, personal communication, February 1978). The two vertical fish near the top of Stela 5 appear to be hung by a strap around the body immediately in front of the tail fin. They bear some resemblance (including the two lateral stripes) to the two fish shown swimming in the water on Stela 67. The fish on Stela 67 have a faint suggestion of a cephalic disk. They may, therefore, bear some resemblance to the shark-sucker *Echeneis naucrates* Linnaeus (Jordan and Evermann 1900: Fig. 796); the band around the tail (as on Stelae 5, 22, and 67) suggests their use for catching fish and turtles (Gudger 1919). The two fish at the bottom of Stela 1 might represent extremely stylized sunfish (Jordan and Evermann 1900: Figs. 424, 426, 427).

All these suggestions are, of course, tenuous, but there appears to be an Izapa interest in marine or brackish rather than freshwater fish.

In addition to their interest in crocodiles, serpents, and fish, the Izapa also represented birds, jaguars, and their characteristics. The birds considered—those on the crocodile's tail in Stela 25, and in the upper right portion of Stela 5—appear to be long-legged, duck-billed marsh birds. Wings (AWING) are given to several figures: those upside down on Stelae 2, 4, and 27; on the falling figure on Stela 60; and on the standing figure on Stela 11. The birdlike figure perched at the top of Stela 25 has been coded as a bird although it is unclear whether this figure is meant to represent the animal or a person wearing an elaborate bird costume. Jaguars are depicted fairly realistically and are shown crouching on Stelae 14, 21, and 22 (where it is missing the head), hung up in a woven net on Stela 12, or sitting in begging fashion on Stela 27.

Animals, and characteristic animal appendages, are:

Code	Description	Izapa stelae and figures in the text
AESER	double-headed earth serpent	5 (Fig. 23a), 7 (Fig. 24b), 11 (Fig. 22a), 12 (Fig. 22b).
ASSER	double-headed sky serpent	7 (Fig. 24a), 18 (Fig. 25b), 23 (Fig. 25a), 26? (Fig. 23b).
ASERP	single-headed serpent	3 (Fig. 21a), 22 (Fig. 8a), 25 (Fig. 26b), 50 (Fig. 5b), 67 (Figs. 8b, 9a).
ABFTM	bifurcated tongue emerging from mouth	3 (Fig. 21a), 6 (Fig. 21c), 7 (Fig. 24a), 18 (Fig. 25b), 23 (Fig. 25a), 26 (Fig. 23b).
ASAPD	serpent head as appendage or clothing	1 (Fig. 6a), 6 (Fig. 11), 50 (Fig. 10a).
ACRFT	crocodile feet	2 (Fig. 39a), 4? (Fig. 15b), 6 (Fig. 11), 11 (Fig. 12a), 25 (Fig. 39b), 60 (Fig. 14c).
AJAGU	jaguar (or feline)	12 (Fig. 22b), 14 (Fig. 27a), 21 (Fig. 27b), 22 (Fig. 34b), 27 (Fig. 27c).
AFISH	fish	1 (Fig. 28c, d), 5 (Fig. 28b), 22 (Fig. 28e), 67 (Fig. 28a).

ABIRD	birds	5 (Fig. 28g), 25 (Figs. 13b, 28h).
AWING	wings worn by the figure	2 (Fig. 14a), 4 (Fig. 15b), 11 (Fig. 16a), 25 (Fig. 13b), 27 (Fig. 14b), 60 (Fig. 14c).
AFINS	fins worn by the figure	1 (Fig. 6a), 5 (Fig. 28f).

Group V: Heads. There are four types of abstract heads that appear without bodies or are attached to other visual elements. A downward-peering head (HDNPR) may be incorporated into the top frame of the scene as on Stela 7, or it may be attached to an anthropomorphic figure as it is on Stela 4. These heads are always presented with the profile face parallel to the picture plane. Because downward-peering heads occur on stelae from other nearby and not-so-near sites—Kaminaljuyu Stela 11 (Miles 1965: Fig. 15a), Tikal Stela 29 (W. R. Coe 1967: 95), Tikal Stela 4 (Miles 1965: Fig. 9d), El Baul Stela 1 (Paddock 1966: Fig. 63), and Abaj Takalik Stela 2 (Miles 1965: Fig. 9a)—Quirarte (1973: 19–20) considers them part of the Izapa stylistic tradition. Miles (1965: 255) briefly discusses the downward-peering head on Kaminaljuyu Stela 11 which she places in Division 3 (or the Late Preclassic or Protoclassic).[4]

The scroll-eyed head (HSEYE) is characterized by a human nose with a long alveolar bar exposed. Sometimes a masklike extension is attached to the front of the nose bar and forehead, thus creating a great upturned or downward moving snout (HDRAG) (Miles 1965: 252). Miles feels that there is a connection between the scroll-eyed heads and water because of the juxtaposition of these two traits on Stelae 1 and 23 (1965: 252). However, because the two opposing bodiless heads with water and/or fish between them are not always scroll-eyed heads, as for example on Stelae 22 and 67, they have been coded separately here (HOPOS).

Long-lipped or dragon heads (HDRAG) are distinguished from scroll-eyed heads in that they may be seen frontally, with a huge down-turned mouth and two eyes (one with pupil and one without), or as dragons in profile with a single eye and exposed mandible. An example of this dragon is found at the base of Stela 2. Quirarte (1973: 19–20) discusses the separate elements of the scroll-eyed head and feels that the scroll forms are serpentine attributes, while the inclusion of the stepped horizontal band as a mouth designates a creature with feline characteristics (Quirarte 1973: Fig. 9a). Quirarte further interprets the dragon or long-lipped heads as terrestrial and celestial symbols.

The types of heads presented are:

[4]Miles's correlations of Sculpture Divisions with Highland Ceramics phases are as follows: Division 1 corresponds to Las Charcas or Arevalo Ceramics and to the Early or Middle Preclassic, 650–450 B.C.; Division 2 corresponds to Providencia Ceramics and to the Middle and late Middle Preclassic, 550–250? B.C.; Division 3 corresponds to the Miraflores Phase and the Late Preclassic and Protoclassic, 300 B.C.–A.D. 1; and Division 4 corresponds to Arenal Ceramics and the Protoclassic or very early Early Classic, 100 B.C.–A.D. 150 (1965: 273).

Code	Description	Izapa stelae and figures in the text
HDNPR	downward-peering head	4 (Fig. 15b), 7 (Fig. 15c).
HSEYE	scroll-eyed head	1 (Fig. 30b), 3 (Fig. 29a), 5 (Fig. 29c), 21 (Fig. 29d), 22 (Fig. 29b), 23 (Fig. 30a), 50 (Fig. 29e).

HDRAG	long-lipped or dragon head	2 (Fig. 32a), 5 (Fig. 32b), 10 (Fig. 32c), 27 (Fig. 32d, h).
HOPOS	opposing, bodiless heads at the base of the scene	1 (Fig. 30b), 22 (Fig. 31c), 23 (Fig. 30a), 67 (Fig. 31b).

Group VI: Glyphs. While it is possible that many of the visual elements are a form of hieroglyph, five have been designated as glyphs because they have a more symbolic and ideographic character than a realistic or representative one. The canoe-shaped U element with a human head (GBOAT) for example, is suggested by Miles (1965: 251–252) to be an early form of the U element (not separately discussed here); Quirarte (1976: 84–85) sees it as an example of the basic U element of design that (in glyphic context) may echo an Olmec influence in the past. This glyph resembles a person sitting in a canoe, particularly in its presentation on Stelae 3 and 26.

The mountain glyph (GMTNS) is described by M. D. Coe (1965: 763) as a step design, "apparently a marker for very late Preclassic sculpture in the Gulf lowlands, in monuments which are obviously Olmec-derived but which follow in time the Olmec style; these include Stela C at Tres Zapotes (where the motif appears on both sides of the mouth), the Alvarado Stela (Covarrubias 1957: Fig. 29), and the rather un-Olmec stelae from Tepatlaxco, Veracruz" (Covarrubias 1957: Pl. 17). Because of its placement in baseline designs, Quirarte interprets this same configuration as a jaguar attribute, or a terrestrial symbol, in Izapa art (1973: 16). The mountain glyph is depicted clearly on Stelae 5 and 12; it is coded as appearing on the badly eroded and damaged Stela 26 (Norman 1976: 137) as well. On Stela 26, the important step design is missing. However, it is likely this design was once present. The triangles are enclosed by a rectangular base panel and have three parallel lines extending across their apexes—both are characteristics of the panel on Stela 5 which is located in the

same row of monuments (see Norman 1976: 137 for a comparative description). The glyph is called "mountain glyph" here simply because of its appearance.

Next, the "jaguar glyph" (GJAGU) is so named because it appears on the head of the jaguar on Stela 12. It also occurs as part of a toponymic glyph at Monte Alban II (Fig. 33e). In addition, a variation of this glyph, lacking only the indentations that give the body of the glyph a clover shape, is found on the head of a stone anthropomorphic jaguar of unknown provenance. M. D. Coe (1973: 25, Pl. 1) supposes this jaguar was carved in or near the Maya area and dates from c. 300 B.C. to A.D. 1.

The Kan-Cross glyph (GKANC) is really a cartouche with the outline of a Kan-Cross (Norman 1973: Pl. 45). Its function may be to designate recession in space. Alternately, it may be a glyph superimposed on the subject presented and function as a label (Kubler 1967: 6) as on the tree of Stela 27. This cartouche serves as a frame for an image placed within its boundaries.

The hill glyph (GHILL) is also a cartouche on Stela 14, but it is simultaneously a headdress shape and a boat on Stelae 22 and 67. This design is described as a stepped element by Norman (1973: Pl. 35) who further identifies it as the outline of a jaguar snout (1976: 48–49). The hill glyph appears on several other monuments at Izapa; most notably, it is the sole design of Miscellaneous Monument 61, Stela 70, and Altar 13 (Norman 1976: Figs. 8.85, 3.46, 5.6). This glyph has been named after the *cerro* or hill glyph at Monte Alban (Caso 1965b: 939–940).

The glyphs are:

Code	Description	*Izapa stelae and figures in the text*
GBOAT	canoe-shaped U element with a human head	3 (Fig. 32e), 6 (Fig. 32f), 26 (Fig. 32g).

GMTNS	mountain glyph, a step design enclosed by diagonal lines which meet at the apex	5 (Fig. 33f), 12 (Fig. 33g), 26 (Fig. 33h).
GJAGU	jaguar glyph, a three-lobed glyph with a bifurcated element emerging from the central lobe	5 (Fig. 33d), 12 (Fig. 33c).
GKANC	a Kan-Cross shaped cartouche	8 (Fig. 33a), 27 (Fig. 33b).
GHILL	a stepped element, as the *cerro* glyph, Monte Alban	14 (Fig. 34a), 22 (Fig. 34b), 67 (Fig. 34c).

Group VII: Objects. This group includes descriptive or abstract images of trees, leaves, weapons or objects held in the hand, incense burners, and water. The images in this group are particularly suited to Panofsky's (1939) description of natural and conventional meanings. Both the formal and the contextual aspects of each image must be examined to understand their meanings. For example, the images of water contribute to the overall sense of movement in the scenes by being depicted as rippling water below (TWBLW), dripping as if upon stalactites (TWABV), or as falling water (TWFAL). The placement of water also contributes to an overall aqueous theme (Stela 1) or it may designate the environment in or upon which the action takes place. The glyph on the extreme central right of Stela 12 has been included here as falling water because stylized water seems to pour from it. It may be compared, as well, to a very similar water-surrounded design on the undated Tres Zapotes Monument C (Stirling 1943: Pls. 17, 18a) (Fig. 36a). Incense burners (TINBR) are identified by Norman (1973: Pl. 39), Miles (1965: 259), and Lowe (1965: 53–64). Along with fire, incense burners are usually associated with seated pairs of figures.

Where they occur, weapons are knives, L-shaped war clubs (TKNIF), or curved staffs (TBATN); these latter may be scepters and therefore symbols of status rather than weapons. The crooked or curved staffs are held outward from the body in a touching gesture that contrasts with the beheading pose found in conjunction with clubs or knives. Nevertheless, Miles believes these curved objects to be a kind of weapon. She describes the "fat nude man" on Stela 10 as being "taken to pieces" by two smaller figures; one of those smaller figures is armed with a staff (1965: 252). Norman (1976: 80–82) suggests that these objects may be both atlatls and scepters, the utilitarian power of the atlatl having been transferred to a more symbolic use. The Izapa knife shown on Stela 21 may be compared to the knife on Bilbao Monument 21 (Parsons 1969, Vol. 2: Pl. 31), but as it occurs only once at Izapa, this knife is included with the clubs for coding purposes. (Norman [1976: Fig. 2.41f] also includes the object, held by the figure seated to the extreme left on Stela 5, as a sacrificial knife; however, the gesture and pose of this figure do not support that interpretation.)

Next, trees are associated with water because they are found emerging from saurian, dragon, or amphibian bases as on Stelae 2, 5, 25, and 27 (TTRDR). Further, regardless of leaf type, the trees often bear fruit (TFRUT), and probably for that reason the tree on Stela 2 is identified by Norman (1973: Pl. 3) as a calabash (*Crescentia cujete*). There are two kinds of tree leaves—the nearly heart-shaped (TTRLA) and the seriated palm, or paddle-shaped (TTRLB).

In Kubler's (1967) model, all of the images called "objects" would occupy nominal and adjectival positions. Objects are:

Code	Description	Izapa stelae and figures in the text
TWBLW	water below, at the base of the scene	1 (Fig. 30b), 5 (Fig. 31a), 22 (Fig. 31c), 23 (Fig. 30a), 67 (Fig. 31b).
TWABV	water above, at the top of the scene	21 (Fig. 35a), 26 (Fig. 35b).
TWFAL	falling water	1 (Fig. 35c), 5 (Fig. 35d), 6 (Fig. 35e), 12 (Fig. 36b), 23 (Figs. 15a, 30a).
TINBR	incense burner or fire	5 (Fig. 37a), 12 (Fig. 37c), 18 (Fig. 37d), 24 (Figs. 10b, 37b).
TKNIF	knife or short, L-shaped club	3 (Fig. 3b), 4 (Fig. 3a), 21 (Fig. 4a).
TBATN	crooked or curved staff	9 (Fig. 5a), 10 (Fig. 4c).
TTRDR	tree-dragon	2 (Fig. 39a), 5 (Fig. 38b), 10 (Fig. 38c), 25 (Fig. 39b), 27 (Fig. 39c).
TTRLA	heart-shaped tree leaves	5 (Fig. 38b), 10 (Fig. 38c), 12 (Fig. 38a), 25 (Fig. 39b), 27 (Fig. 39c).
TTRLB	seriated palm or paddle-shaped tree leaves	2 (Fig. 39a), 27 (Fig. 39c).
TFRUT	fruit	2 (Fig. 39a), 5 (Fig. 38b), 27 (Fig. 27c).
TBLUD	blood	12 (Fig. 22b), 21 (Fig. 13a), 25 (Fig. 8c).

Groups VIII and IX: Jewelry and Clothing. Jewelry and clothing may be worn by human, animal, or anthropomorphic figures. The types of jewelry are analyzed for their usefulness in comparing otherwise related Izapa figures (Proskouriakoff 1950: 82–85) and the Izapa figures with those appearing on stelae from other archaeological sites. The ornaments may be simple rounded beads worn as a necklace (CNEKL) or band-type anklets or bracelets (CANKW).

Although there are only three characteristics listed here under clothing—the stiff cloak (CCLOK), the bifurcated tongue as the end of a belt, loincloth tie, or perhaps phallus (CTBLT), and knee-pads (CBPPD)—the last two are surely significant to the meaning of the stelae. The bifurcated tongue that appears on the loincloth tie is the same type that emerges from the mouth of the serpent on Stela 3. These serpent images iden-

tify the figure with the abstract serpent-jaguar topline design and thereby help to unite the composition while adding importance to the person or deity represented. The wearer of knee-pads may be related to the ball game.[5] The stiff cloak (identified by Miles [1965: 255] as a "stiff hide cape") is most likely an example of Olmec influence. From his survey of its various representa-

[5]Norman (1976: 153) discusses the association of the figure wearing knee-pads with the ball game, particularly in the context of Stela 60. As evidence he cites the position of the stela at the end field of the ball court, and compares the images in general to the mythical ball game in the Popol Vuh. The subject and composition of Stela 60 are compared to a Late or Middle Classic stela at El Baul (Norman 1976: Fig. 6.10) that is most certainly a depiction of ball players. As Norman himself notes, however, Stela 60 was probably moved from its original placement (Norman 1976: 152) and the other stelae that depict ball player pads (Stelae 1, 3, and 7) were not positioned near the ball court. Thus, there are possible, but not certain, associations between this part of Izapa costume and the ball game.

tions, Drucker (1981: 34) makes the inference that the Olmec cloaks were status symbols and were made of hide (perhaps jaguar with pelage), of cotton cloth, or were feather-covered. Such cloaks are worn by three figures on Tres Zapotes Stela D (Fig. 50).

Jewelry and clothing are:

Code	Description	Izapa stelae and figures in the text
CNEKL	rounded beads worn as a necklace	5 (Figs. 6b, 17a), 18 (Fig. 17a), 21 (Figs. 4a, 13a), 24 (Fig. 17d).
CANKW	band-type anklets or bracelets	1 (Fig. 6a), 2 (Fig. 6d), 4 (Fig. 3a), 5 (Fig. 17b, c), 6 (Fig. 11), 11 (Fig. 12a), 12 (Fig. 17f), 24 (Figs. 10b, 17d), 25 (Fig. 39b), 67 (Fig. 9a).
CTBLT	bifurcated tongue belt or tie	2 (Fig. 6d), 3 (Fig. 3b), 4 (Fig. 3a), 23 (Fig. 15a).
CBPPD	knee-pads	1 (Fig. 6a), 3 (Fig. 3b), 7 (Fig. 7b), 60 (Fig. 7a).
CCLOK	stiff cloak	9 (Fig. 5a), 50 (Fig. 5b).

Classification and Interpretation

Classification: Cluster Analysis

Having identified and defined the various visual elements or traits found regularly on the Izapa stelae, I then analyzed the traits statistically. This part of the analysis is designed to discover which traits regularly co-occur as well as the groups they form. The groups of traits may be stated as formulae, or rules for design; they are the basis for the argument that there is an Izapa iconography. Such groups of traits may also be used to cluster stelae.

To determine the degree of association between traits, and among any groups these traits might form, a cluster analysis procedure is used. A basic review of the procedure for cluster analysis, a technique developed by biologists to define taxonomic units, is presented in *Principles of Numerical Taxonomy* (Sokal and Sneath 1963). A computer program NT-SYS, *Numerical Taxonomy System of Multivariate Statistical Programs* (Rohlf et al. 1974), is used to make the calculations for the clustering procedure. The calculations in NT-SYS are taken directly from Sokal and Sneath. The procedure applied to these data is as follows.

Statistical comparisons are made to measure the frequency of occurence of each pair of visual traits. First, the individual stelae are coded according to the presence or absence of particular visual traits (Fig. 51), with the focus being upon nominal comparisons. Recording the data as nominal (present/absent) ignores multiple occurrences, on any stela, of a particular trait. The number of times a trait appears on a single stela is not important in this analysis; the interest lies in which traits occur together. Negative matches (absent traits matched with absent traits) are omitted from consideration. By omitting these matches, a source of error is deleted, for a particular absence may be due to damage or erosion of a stela. Since the association of traits and the similarity of stelae is determined by traits being present together, to include in the calculations the relatively high number of co-occurring absences would obscure these relationships.

Because the data are nominal, and because of the relatively large number of absences, the coefficient of Jaccard (Sokal and Sneath 1963: 133) is chosen. Jaccard is a similarity coefficient that omits consideration of negative matches. This formula is expressed as

$$\frac{A}{(N-D)}$$

where A is the number of positive (present/present) matches between traits, N is the total number of possible matches (present/present + present/absent + absent/present + absent/absent), and D is the number of negative (absent/absent) matches. Thus the number of positive matches is divided by the total possible number minus the common absences. This formula is an option in the "SIMQUAL" routine of NT-SYS and can be used to produce an association matrix in which each trait (or variable) is compared with every other trait. The analysis produces coefficients ranging from 0.0 (no association) to 1.0 (perfect association).

The traits are then clustered according to their degree of association. A *complete linkage* procedure (Sokal and Sneath 1963: 181) is executed by the "TAXON" routine of NT-SYS. The "TAXON" procedure first clusters the variables with the highest coefficients of association. These clusters are then linked at progressively lower levels of association. The process continues until all of the traits have been grouped into clusters. The similarity between two clusters is governed by the lowest association between *any* item in one cluster and any item in the other cluster, regardless of how highly associated other inter-cluster pairs may be. Thus, the procedure is called *complete linkage* because ultimately all clusters are combined into one. Whether or not the clusters "make sense" is a subjective decision of the investigator, based on knowledge of the data and the level of association (the Jaccard coefficient in this case) assigned to the clusters.

This type of analysis is also used to cluster the stelae, with the Jaccard coefficients computed between pairs of stelae. These coefficients of similarity for the stelae are based on the number of traits they both share relative to the total number of traits present on at least one of the two stelae. In this part of the analysis the original data matrix is turned on its side as a basis for generating a new array of coefficients. The computer's results of these analyses of traits and of stelae are presented by the dendograms shown in Tables 1 and 2.

Classification: Variables or Visual Traits

The variables dendogram (Table 2, see also Table 1) shows the clusters of traits and their levels of association. These levels are presented by the duplicate scales printed at the top and bottom of the dendogram, which also allow observation of overall patterns of related traits. The exact coefficient of association between a trait and the one listed just beneath it may be read at the right of each code. The clusters of traits suggested by the dendogram and chosen for this analysis are indicated in the far right column.

The primary clusters, or those with the highest levels of association, are composed of only two variables each. They are DBEHD (beheading pose) and TKNIF (knife, or short, L-shaped club) in Trait Group 6, GMTNS (mountain glyph) and GJAGU (jaguar glyph) in Trait Group 9, and ABIRD (birds) with TTRLA (heart-shaped tree leaves) in Trait Group 10. Such small clusters are not sufficient to interpret themes or meanings expressed in Izapa art. On the other hand, if we look at clusters associated at the minimum level of 0.2000, there is a much better basis for inter-

pretation. However, these judgments must be qualified on the strength of association of smaller clusters with higher levels of association. At the 0.2000 level, there are eleven clusters of at least three visual traits each. These are the trait groups that are indicated on the variables dendogram and numbered from top to bottom. These groups are first described and then examined for the Izapa themes they present.

Trait Group 1 includes seven visual traits that are figure-poses or arrangements of picture ground. Traits in Group 1 are:

FSTAN   standing figure
FLARG   large figure
SPLAN   shallow spatial depth
SOVER   overlapping of figures
FSTIN   seated individual figure
FFRRP   figure fractionally represented
SVERT   vertical perspective

Thus on an Izapa stela where there is shallow spatial depth (often with figures standing on a groundline) the occurrence of a standing figure and a large figure is quite likely. A seated individual may be present, at least one figure will be fractionally represented, and there may be some use of vertical perspective as well. In addition, overlapping of figures is likely to occur. This group of traits is best seen by Stelae 21, 22, 50, 60, and 67 which show all the traits in Group 1. Stelae 10 and 11 are missing the use of vertical perspective only. Stela 2 has all traits in the group except a seated individual, while Stela 5 does not include fractional representation. Three traits in Trait Group 1—the large figure, a seated individual, and shallow spatial depth (coefficient of association 0.585)—occur on five other stelae, Stelae 6, 7, 8, 24, and 27.

Trait Group 2 also consists of figure-pose and picture ground traits. They are:

FPROF   figure represented in profile or three-quarter view
FSMAL   small figure
SSYMT   if one figure, central placement and bilateral symmetry; if two or more figures, equal placement from the center

From Trait Group 2 it can be seen that small figures are usually represented in profile or three-quarter view. In addition, the presence of these two traits indicates a symmetrical arrangement of the figure or figures in space. Further, Group 2 traits are linked to Trait Group 1 at a minimum level of 0.2941. All three traits in Trait Group 2 occur on Stelae 2, 5, 8, 9, 12, 14, 18, and 22. On Stelae 10 and 24, a small figure occurs with a figure represented in profile or three-quarter view, although on Stela 10 the large seated figure is shown in profile. On Stela 23 the arrangement of figures in space is symmetrical, and all of the figures are shown in profile or three-quarter view.

The next group of traits, Trait Group 3, includes:

DWRST   holding or wrestling a serpent
ASERP   a single-headed serpent
AFISH   fish
TWBLW   water below, or at the base of the scene
HOPOS   opposing, bodiless heads at the base of the scene
HSEYE   scroll-eyed heads

Where there are fish, water is represented at the base of the scene. These two traits are juxtaposed on Stelae 1, 5, 22, and 67 although on Stela 5 the fish are not placed in the water. Opposing bodiless heads that may or may not be scroll-eyed (coefficient of association 0.3750) are also likely to occur where there is water below. This juxtaposition may be seen on Stelae 1, 22, 23, and 67. Also, where there is a serpent, it is probably wrestled, attacked, or wound about another figure, as for example on Stelae 22, 25, and 50 (and possibly 67). It should be noted that on Stela 3 the serpent is not only being attacked, but being beheaded. On Stela 1, above the topline design (and therefore not coded), a person handles a serpent. Only on Stela 22 do all six traits in this group occur. The group, nevertheless, remains fairly cohesive; on Stelae 5, 23, 50, and 67 in addition to Stela 22 (which has all traits), at least three of the six traits in Group 3 occur in various combinations. Finally, Trait Group 3 is slightly related to Trait Group 2 with a coefficient of association of 0.1111.

Trait Group 4 contains three traits:

FPRST   pair of seated figures
TINBR   incense burners or fire
CNEKL   necklace of rounded beads

These three traits are associated at a minimum level of 0.6000 although the relationship between the seated pair of figures and the incense burner of fire is stronger and is 0.8000. On Stelae 5, 18, and 24 all three traits occur; however, on Stela 12 the rounded bead necklace is absent or unobservable. This group of traits is cohesive, with a high level of association. Since it does not have a statistical relationship with the other groups of traits, though, the occurrence of Trait Group 4 should not be considered dependent upon the presence of another cluster.

The next group, Trait Group 5, consists of the following traits:

FFODV   falling or diving figure
CTBLT   bifurcated tongue as belt or loincloth tie
SABBL   picture plane divided into two regions vertically, as figures stand on or emerge from, top- and baseline designs
AWING   figure wearing wings
ACRFT   crocodile feet

In this group the falling or diving figure, the bifurcated tongue as a loincloth tie or belt, and picture plane divided into upper and lower regions are associated at 0.6000. Wings and reptilian or crocodile feet (associated at 0.7143) are loosely joined to the first three traits at a minimum level of 0.2857. On Stelae 2 and 4 all traits in this group are present. Figures on Stelae 11, 25, and 60 have crocodile feet and wings; while the winged figure on Stela 60 does not fall or dive, his crumpled legs give him the appearance of having already fallen. Stela 27 has a falling winged figure too, but as this figure is very small and contained within a cartouche, it is not possible to determine if other traits in the group are present. Trait Group 5 is related to the next group of traits, Group 6, at the very low level of 0.1250.

The sixth group of visual traits is:

DBEHD beheading pose
TKNIF knife or club
HDNPR downward-peering head

While there is a perfect relationship (1.0000) between the figure posed as if to behead someone and a knife or club, these two traits are clustered with the downward-peering head at the 0.3333 level. The downward-peering head on Stela 4 belongs to the falling figure and is not disembodied as is the head on Stela 7. Because there is no knife, club, or beheading pose on Stela 7, the downward-peering head ought not to be considered an important member of this trait group. On Stelae 3, 4, and 21 the beheading pose and a knife or club co-occur. Trait Group 6 is related only to Trait Group 5.

Trait Group 7 is another small cluster of visual traits:

DCHLD carrying a child or small person on the back
CCLOK stiff cloak
TBATN crooked or curved staff

Because each of these traits occurs only twice it is significant that all three traits appear on Stela 9. However, as Trait Group 7 is not related to the other groups and because these traits occur so infrequently, this group may not be important in identifying the Izapa art style. It is significant that the idea of holding or carrying a child in a ceremonial context, the staff, and the cloak are traits that also occur in Olmec art.

Trait Group 8 includes three traits:

DMOTH holding something on the tongue or in the mouth
ABFTM bifurcated tongue emerging from the mouth
GBOAT canoe-shaped U element with human head

On Stelae 3 and 6 a canoe-shaped U element with a human head is balanced on a bifurcated tongue that emerges from the mouth of a crea-ture. On Stela 26, bifurcated tongues project from the mouths of a double-headed sky serpent, but the two canoe-shaped glyphs are not balanced on these tongues. Further, bifurcated tongues occur frequently on the Izapa stelae and protrude from the mouths of serpents on Stelae 7, 18, and 23. Trait Group 8 is associated with one other trait, ASAPD (a serpent head as an appendage), but this coefficient is only 0.1667. Such a low level of association reflects the fact that in only one of three cases (on Stela 6) does this element appear with the three traits in Group 8. Trait Group 8 is not related to any other trait groups. Trait Group 9 includes six traits:

AESER double-headed earth serpent
GMTNS mountain glyph, a step design enclosed by diagonal lines which meet at the apex
GJAGU jaguar glyph, a three-lobed glyph with a bifurcated element emerging from the central lobe
CANKW band-type anklets or bracelets
TWFAL falling water
AFINS fins as attached appendages

The closest relationships within this group are among the first three traits: the double-headed earth serpent, the mountain glyph, and the jaguar glyph. Weakly linked to these traits are the band-type anklets or bracelets, falling water, and attached fins. All of the traits in Group 9 occur on Stela 5, and Stela 12 includes all traits except the attached fins. Stelae 1 and 6 share two traits from the group, the band-type jewelry and falling water. Even though the jaguar glyph is represented only twice, it is notable that it co-occurs with four other traits in Group 9. Fins also appear only twice, but they contribute to reinforce the water theme (specified as falling water) in this group. Finally, Trait Group 9 is associated with Trait Group 10 at a minimum level of 0.1111.

Trait Group 10 is another three-trait cluster:

ABIRD birds
TTRLA heart-shaped tree leaves
TTRDR tree-dragon

The three traits in this group are all present on Stelae 5 and 25. The only other instances of birds might be the creatures or persons who seem to be wearing their wings. Heart-shaped tree leaves and the tree-dragon are present together on Stela 10, however. The tree-dragon is featured in conjunction with a diving or falling winged figure on Stelae 2 and 27. Therefore, the connection between bird forms and tree-dragons may be stronger than the statistics indicate.

Trait Group 11 consists of:

TTRLB palm or paddle-shaped tree leaves
TFRUT fruit
HDRAG long-lipped or dragon head

The palm or paddle-shaped leaves, fruit, and the dragon head all occur on Stelae 2 and 27. Dragon heads are usually shown at the base of a tree, thus connecting this group of traits with Trait Group 10. However, on Stela 2 this head is repeated as the headdress of the falling figure. On Stela 4 the dragon head serves only as a headdress motif. Also, fruit may grow on a dragon tree with heart-shaped leaves as it does on Stela 5, thus pointing to a connection between Trait Group 11 and Trait Group 10.

In addition to these groups of traits, there are four pairs that do not cluster with the other visual elements but have coefficients of association of at least 0.2500. (These pairs of traits are indicated on Table 2 by the brackets between Trait Groups 3 and 4, 8 and 9, 10 and 11, and after Trait Group 11.) These traits are: the jaguar (AJAGU) and the hill glyph (GHILL), the serpent head as an appendage (ASAPD) and knee-pads (CBPPD), water above (TWABV) and blood (TBLUD), and the Kan-Cross glyph (GKANC) and the representation of recessional depth (SRECS). The jaguar and the hill glyph occur on Stelae 14 and 22. There are jaguars on Stelae 12, 21, and 27 as well, and there may be a jaguar perched on the hill glyph of Stela 67. (Unfortunately, the upper part of Stela 67 is missing.) These two traits are linked to Trait Group 3 at the 0.1053 level. The serpent as an appendage and the knee-pads share a coefficient of 0.2500 but appear together only on Stela 1. Knee-pads, which are apparently only slightly associated with any other traits, are worn by figures on Stelae 3, 7, and 60. These two traits are linked to Trait Group 8 with a coefficient of 0.1667. Water above (or at the top of the scene) and blood appear together at the 0.2500 level and only on Stela 21. Although these traits are represented only two and three times respectively, they contribute to an analysis of Izapa art as they are unique to that site. Finally, the Kan-Cross glyph and recessional depth are associated at the 0.6667 level. There is only one instance of the use of recessional depth without the Kan-Cross glyph—on Stela 14. These two traits are related to Trait Group 11, and therefore to Group 10, with a coefficient of association of 0.1667.

Interpretation: Groups of Visual Traits

The ten groups and four pairs of associated visual traits are the rules for the use of visual elements in Izapa art. By their frequent co-occurrence, these traits combine to express a limited number of particular themes or meanings. These themes are now discussed and interpreted as they appear on individual stelae.

Trait Groups 1 and 2 most obviously indicate the rules for the size and pose of the figures as well as their arrangement in space. There is an overall relationship between the size and importance of the figure and whether or not it is posed in profile, three-quarter view, or fractionally represented. As can be seen on Stelae 3, 4, 11, 21, 22, and 67, large figures (standing or seated) are usually fractionally represented if there is also shallow spatial depth with the figures standing on a groundline (Figs. 3a, b, 4a, 9a, b, 12a, 16a). Winged figures, figures posed as if to behead someone, and seated figures with arms extended in winglike fashion (Stelae 22 and 67) are also fractionally represented (Figs. 9a, 9b). Where vertical perspective is employed, the small figures are fractionally represented only if the composition is not symmetrical, as occurs on Stela 21 (Fig. 4a). Most small figures are shown in profile and in conjunction with a symmetrical composition as on Stelae 2, 5, 12, 14, 18, and 24 (Figs. 6b–d, 10b, 17a–f). There are three large figures shown in profile that are also standing or sitting on a groundline: the figure on Stela 1, the largest figure on Stela 27, and the skeletal figure on Stela 50 (Figs. 6a, 7c, 10a). None of these compositions is symmetrical. As can be seen on Stelae 6, 7, 9, 25, and 60, large figures that are not supported by a groundline are frequently portrayed in profile or three-quarter view (Figs. 5a, 7a, b, 8c, 11, 13b). Overlapping of figures to show spatial depth is a characteristic of Izapa art that is associated with all types of figures and poses.

Trait Group 3 provides a connection between the realm of water, opposing heads, and serpents. For example, the opposing bodiless heads occur only in the context of being separated by flowing water. Two of these pairs of heads are scroll-eyed, as on Stelae 1 and 23 (Figs. 30a, b). Other scroll-eyed heads appear in water, as shown on Stela 1, or as heads of serpents, as illustrated by Stelae 3, 5, 22, and 50 (Figs. 29a–c, e). On Stela 21, a scroll-eyed head is part of a headdress (Fig. 29d), but the connection is with water since the figure stands below falling water. The representation of scroll-eyed heads along with fish on Stelae 1, 5, and 22 (the portion of Stela 67 which might have scroll-eyed heads is missing) also confirms their connection to water.

Serpents, too, are representatives of water. In addition to some serpents having scroll-eyed heads, they actually emerge from water on Stelae 22 and 67 (Figs. 8a, b, 9a) (and perhaps on Stela 5 if the double-headed serpent can be viewed as extending to the level of the water). Serpents are part of the costume or anatomy of the figure standing over water on Stela 1 (Fig. 6a). One might supose that these serpents are viewed as creatures to be overcome by someone above the water. On Stela 3 a serpent is beheaded, and on Stela 50 a serpent or serpent-umbilicus is wrestled (Figs. 5b, 10a). Also, a serpent reaches upward and around a small figure on the right of Stela 67 (Fig. 8b). While this motif is repeated on Stela 22

(Fig. 8a), the central figure is grasping serpents in both hands (Fig. 9b). Finally, on Stela 1 above the topline design a figure handles a writhing serpent (Fig. 26a).

Trait Group 4 indicates that in Izapa art seated opposing figures are generally attendants of incense burners or fire (Fig. 17b, d–f). Certainly no incense burner is unattended, although on Stela 24 one *incensario* has a single observer (Fig. 10b). At the lower left of Stela 5, there is a seated pair of figures with a childlike personage between them (Fig. 17c). These figures may be a scribe-priest and an assistant since the larger of the two figures holds a possible writing tool in his left hand. Norman (1976: 190) suggests that the childlike figure is a "real or symbolic burial bundle (or readied child sacrifice)." If Norman's suggestion is correct, the placement of a human offering between two seated figures parallels in meaning the incense offered by two attendants in the lower right carving on the same stela. The presence of the rounded bead necklace worn by the pairs of figures on Stelae 5, 18, and 24 (Figs. 6b, 17c, a, d) might be a further identification of those with the role of attendant; however, this necklace is also worn by the large figures on Stela 21 (Figs. 4a, 13a) and is not visible on Stela 12.

The fifth group of visual traits suggests that there is a connection between winged figures (who sometimes descend dramatically from the sky) and serpents or reptiles. First, winged figures appear on Stelae 2, 4, 11, 25, 27, and 60. The winged figure on Stela 2 has a simplified version of a bifurcated-tongue belt and wears a dragon headdress (Fig. 14a). He appears above a dragon-based tree and is flanked by two small figures wearing bifurcated-tongue loincloth ties (Fig. 6d). In addition, the falling figure's feet may have curved reptilian toes as a reference to the dragon below. On Stela 4 the descending winged figure again wears a simplified version of the bifurcated-tongue tie, and as on Stela 2, the feet may be reptilian (although avian feet are likely as well) (Fig. 15b). The figure shown standing on Stela 4 wears wings and has a bifurcated-tongue belt tie

(Fig. 3a). He wears a headdress so similar (in outline) to the headgear worn by the winged figure on Stela 2, that it is fairly safe to assume the headdress to be a dragon head. Stelae 11 and 25 provide two more examples of the combination of avian and reptilian characteristics. For instance, Stela 11 has a winged figure standing in or emerging from a squatting reptilian monster (Figs. 16a, 12a). While no bifurcated-tongue ties are present, the squatting figure has knobbed, saurian knees, reptilian feet and hands, and the elongated jaws of a crocodile; he sits on a double-headed serpent. On Stela 25 a figure that looks less like a real bird than a costumed, masked creature wearing wings (Fig. 13b) perches on top of a staff or tree around which winds a serpent (Fig. 26b). The serpent also wraps around a crocodile whose tail becomes tree branches (Fig. 39b). Yet another bird, perhaps a marsh bird because of its long legs and duck bill, is perched on the crocodile's tree-tail (Fig. 28h).

Stela 60 presents another version of the avian-reptilian combined traits. Here, a winged figure with crumpled legs appears at the lower left of the scene (Fig. 14c). This figure has vestiges of what is probably a bifurcated-tongue belt tie and reptilian feet (the foot on the right has five toes) and appears to have fallen or collapsed. Because of the condition of the stela, it is impossible to tell if the two other figures wear wings. The figure to the extreme right, however, possibly wears a bifurcated-tongue belt tie (which remains only partly visible) (Fig. 7a).

Next, on Stela 27 a falling or diving winged figure is shown, enclosed by a cartouche, recessed in a tree with a dragon-head base (Figs. 14b, 39c). The diagonal striations on the trunk of the tree may be a winding serpent, but there are no other indications of the presence of a snake. Below the groundline there is an additional dragon (Fig. 32h). Furthermore, on Stela 23 a figure plunges downward towards the water below (Fig. 15a). While this figure does not wear wings, there are two bifurcated-tongue ties, one at the front and another at the back of his waist.

This figure is framed by a double-headed serpent (Fig. 25a) and hurls something, perhaps thunderbolts or rain, into the splashing, peaked water below (Fig. 30a).

On all of these stelae (Stelae 2, 4, 11, 25, 27, and 60) birds or bird characteristics are seen in conjunction with saurian and serpentine traits. In most cases, a winged figure, or as on Stela 23 a figure without wings, falls or dives from above towards water. Each of these figures is depicted below or next to a creature associated with water, a serpent. Since the connection between avian and reptilian creatures is as consistent as that between reptilian feet, serpents, and scroll-eyed heads, it is possible to interpret the diving or winged figures as rain deities of some sort.

The next group, Trait Group 6, is related to, and aids in, the interpretation of Trait Group 5. Each figure is posed as if to behead; on Stelae 3, 4, and 21 each one also holds a knife or a club (Figs. 3a, b, 4a). Water, or traits strongly associated with water, appear with the beheading pose. For example, the figure with a club on Stela 3 is about to behead a serpent with scroll-eyed heads (Fig. 21a). On Stela 4, a figure with a dragon headdress, bifurcated-tongue belt tie, and wings poses as if to behead either an unseen victim or perhaps the diving figure (Figs. 3a, 15b). Also, on Stela 21 a figure wearing a scroll-eyed headdress stands beneath dripping or falling water (Figs. 4a, 35a). This figure remains posed as if to behead, although he already holds the victim's severed head in his right hand. The third trait in Group 6 is the downward-peering head; it is the downward-facing head of the diving or falling figure on Stela 4 (Fig. 15b) and is therefore associated in this instance with the downward-plunging action. That the downward-peering head is an abbreviated way of representing a diving god may be inferred from its connection to the diving figure on Stela 4 and by its appearance on the upper portion of Stela 7 (Figs. 15c, 55e). Quirarte (1973: 26) suggests that the downward-peering head on Kaminaljuyu Stela 11 (Fig. 41b) is indeed an abbreviated flying figure, saying that in this case, "crossed bands within a large car-touche may very well depict the outstretched wing." The poses of the right-hand pair of fig-ures on Stela 7 are nearly identical to those on Stela 60 (Fig. 7a, b) where the fallen winged fig-ure dominates the lower portion of the scene (Fig. 14c).

Trait Group 7 is not frequently represented on Izapa stelae. The three components of this group, the crooked or curved staff (Fig. 4a, c), the hide cloak (Fig. 5a, b), and carrying a child on the back (Figs. 5a, 6c), appear together only on Stela 9 (Fig. 5a). While this group of traits may not be particularly useful in identifying art that is Izapa, it may be the best example of those traits that are Olmec-derived. For example, La Venta Stela 2 (Bernal 1969: Pl. 17) clearly shows a large central figure wearing a stiff cloak and holding a scepter or staff. The minor figures also carry these ob-jects. If the scepter held by the large figure were held with the arm extended, it would be very similar to those on Izapa Stelae 9 and 10. Stela 3 from La Venta (Fig. 47) also represents two large figures wearing cloaks (although these cloaks are mid-calf length). The figure on the left, and per-haps the figure on the right as well, carry what are likely to be scepters or staves (see Drucker et al. 1959: Figs. 67, 68). Further, there are no Ol-mec representations of a child being carried on the back, although small people or children are frequently held in other poses within a ceremo-nial context. For instance, the large figures on the north and south sides of La Venta Altar 5 (Bernal 1969: Pl. 13b, c) (Fig. 48a, b) are holding smaller persons while wearing cloaks or capes. The Izapa and Olmec poses with children are very different variations of a theme. If there is a significant comparison to be made here, it is the depiction in general of cloaked figures holding children or in-fants in a ceremonial context.

Trait Group 7, then, is a continuance of three related Olmec traits; that the traits maintain their relationship over time suggests that a concept and, to a lesser extent, forms (the cloak and staff) have survived in Izapa art. A definition of this concept

can only be suggested. Whether the small persons or children are being offered as sacrifices (Caso 1965c: 23) is debatable as there are no scenes of children actually being slain; nevertheless, small persons are carried by figures dignified by their cloaks and/or scepters. Also, that the Izapa could participate in violent behavior is shown by the decapitation on Stela 21 (Fig. 13a) and the ampu-tated arm of the figure on Stela 25 (Fig. 8c). At both Izapa and La Venta the small persons are offered or presented by a special individual. The Izapa context for this ritual is unknown on Stela 9, but on Stela 5 there is an overwhelming detail of offerings via incense, the fertility or abundance of the fruit-laden tree, and the many references to water.

Trait Group 8 reinforces and adds to the con-nection between serpents and water, the subject of Trait Group 1. The canoe-shaped U element with a human head (Fig. 32e–g) always appears in the context of water. It may balance on a bi-furcated tongue, as on Stela 3 and 6 (Fig. 21a, c), or as on Stela 26, it may be placed between the bifurcated tongues of a double-headed serpent and beneath falling or dripping water. The fig-ures on Stelae 22 and 67 are shown in boats on the water from which serpents emerge (Fig. 9a, b), and Izapa Miscellaneous Monument 2 (Nor-man 1973: Pl. 64) shows a figure emerging from, or being swallowed by, a huge serpentine head. These figures, in addition to the winged figure on Stela 11 that emerges from a saurian (Figs. 12a, 16a) (also a water-dwelling creature), support a hypothesis that water-associated serpents give forth a deity or priest. The presentation of the converse, that a person is being swallowed, is less likely, for the direction of the action is outward. Further, on Stela 11 the winged figure's out-stretched arms and upward furling wings indicate that he is emerging from the mouth of the sau-rian. Perhaps this scene is another expression of the water giving forth a deity. However, this winged figure is unique in the context of emerg-ing in some way from the mouth of a monster (see Norman 1973: Pl. 22).

Trait Group 9 links together the mountain and jaguar glyphs, falling water, fins, and the band-type anklet or bracelet. Most clearly related are the two glyphs. The jaguar and mountain glyphs occur together twice, on Stelae 5 and 12 (Fig. 33c, d, f, g). While the mountain glyph is indicated at the base of Stela 26 (Fig. 33h), the upper portion is too badly eroded to determine if the jaguar glyph was present as well. Since the jaguar glyph is placed on the head of the jaguar on Stela 12 (Fig. 33c) and occurs on the back of a small carved jaguar from the Maya area (M. D. Coe 1973: Pl. 1), it is possible that the glyph is a reference to this creature. If so, one could venture that the jaguar, not just the jaguar glyph, is associated with the mountain glyph. Strong support for this argument comes from Tres Zapotes Stela C (M. D. Coe 1965: Fig. 42) where the mountain glyph appears on both sides of the mouth of an abstract jaguar mask. Bernal (1969: 62) identifies this mask as Cocijo, the Zapotec rain god. Two other occurrences of the mountain glyph outside the Izapa area are the Alvarado Stela (Covarrubias 1957: Fig. 29) and the stela from Tepatlaxco, Veracruz (Covarrubias 1957: Pl. 17). Neither of these stelae contains the jaguar glyph, but the mountain glyph functions as it does at Izapa, as a baseline design.

At Izapa, the mountain and jaguar glyphs are never present without some representation of water and a double-headed serpent. On Stela 5 water is shown as falling (Fig. 35d), but it is also represented directly below the mountain glyph (Fig. 31a); the double-headed serpent originates in this area (Fig. 23a). On Stela 12, falling water is shown by the design to the right of the double-headed serpent (Fig. 36b). Falling water may be indicated by the flowing scrolls on the extreme right on Stela 26 (Norman 1973: Pl. 44). While this stela apparently has no double-headed earth serpent (or serpent emerging from below), such a serpent occurs at the top of the carving (Fig. 23b) where water drips or falls downward (Fig. 35b).

Falling water appears on Stela 6 with only one other trait in this group—the band-type anklet or bracelet (Fig. 11). Although there are no mountain or jaguar glyphs or double-headed serpents on this stela, a reference to the serpent is made by the serpent tail of the monster. On Stela 1 the same traits are united along with the representation of fins, which appear on the legs and arms of the standing figure (Fig. 6a). Fins occur once more on Stela 5 (Fig. 28f) where all of the traits in the group are present. Additionally, since the band-type anklets or bracelets are shown alone on Stelae 2, 4, 25, and 67, they are not one of the most important elements of this trait group.

From Trait Group 9 it may be determined that the jaguar glyph (if not the jaguar itself), the mountain glyph, falling water, and the double-headed earth serpent are meaningfully related. As has already been shown, serpents in general are related to water. The presence of these glyphs seems to specify falling water and indicates that the jaguar has a role in bringing rainfall.

A theme centered on trees, dragons, and birds is presented by Trait Group 10. Where a tree-dragon occurs, there is a bird, specifically a marsh bird, or a figure wearing an avian costume. This juxtaposition occurs on Stelae 2 (Figs. 39a, 14a), 5 (Figs. 38b, 28g), 25 (Figs. 39b, 13b, 28h), and 27 (Figs. 39c, 14b). Apparently no bird form is shown with the tree-dragon on Stela 10 (Fig. 38c), but this stela is too badly damaged to be certain of that absence. The heart-shaped tree leaf does not always occur on the dragon-tree. On Stela 12 this leaf type is shown on the branches from which are suspended the jaguar (Figs. 22b, 38a), and on Stela 25 the human figure has these leaves in his headdress (Fig. 8c).

The tree-dragon is also associated with water in several ways. For instance, the dragon itself is connected with water. There are knobbed knees, fleshy legs, and froglike feet on the dragon of Stela 2 (Fig. 39a); on Stela 5 water seems to pour from the dragon's head below which more water is represented (Fig. 38b). The dragon on Stela 25 is, in part, a realistically represented crocodile with a conch shell on its nose (Fig. 39b). Another connection with water is the frequent presence of a falling (or diving) figure or a marsh bird. Marsh birds, for example, occur on Stelae 5 and 25. A falling, winged figure is represented directly above the tree-dragon of Stela 2 (Fig. 14a) and on the trunk of the tree on Stela 27 (Fig. 14b).

Trait Group 11 is comprised of the palm or paddle-shaped tree leaves, fruit, and long-lipped or dragon heads. This cluster further defines and reinforces the tree-dragon theme of the previous group. All of the traits in Group 11 occur on Stelae 2 and 27 where a falling figure and a tree-dragon are also present. The connection between tree-dragons and falling or diving winged figures is emphasized by the dragon-head headdress worn by the diving figure on Stela 2 (Fig. 32a). The same headdress is faintly visible on Stela 4 where it is worn by the standing winged figure. Further, not all trees with a dragon base bear fruit, but fruit occurs only in the context of a dragon. The dragon-tree of Stela 2 has fruit and palm-shaped leaves (Fig. 39a). On Stela 27 where this leaf type appears, the fruit is given to or taken from a jaguar (Figs. 39c, 27c). Fruit is also depicted on Stela 5 where the dragon-tree has heart-shaped leaves (Fig. 38b), and its fruit is given to fish (Fig. 28f). As jaguars, dragons, and fish are all associated with water, and as two of these tree-dragons have leaves of the type found in marshy or wet environments, the connection between the tree-dragon and water is reinforced.

An analysis of Trait Groups 10 and 11 shows that tree-dragons are strongly associated with birds and winged figures. Both traits are associated with water. As the tree rises from its dragon-water base, a bird form dives from above, or in the case of Stela 27, a jaguar takes or gives fruit. The overall associations of these figures with water suggests the theme of water falling from above to nourish the life springing from the water below—the result is abundance (fruit). Further evidence for the water-bearing role of the diving or falling figure is given by the wingless but upside-down figure on Stela 23 (Fig. 15a). This figure delivers rain and/or thunderbolts to the water below (Fig. 30a). On Stela 5

the duck-billed, winged figures do not dive, but the figure on the left side of the tree dispenses fruit (Fig. 28f). On Stela 4 a winged figure dives towards another who stands and wears a dragon headdress (Figs. 15b, 3a).

The major themes presented on these Izapa stelae can be summarized and some generalizations made. First, there is certainly an overall expression of concern for water. The creatures or animals regularly represented—the jaguars, the crocodile-dragon, the various serpents, the fish, the birds, and winged figures—are all attached to water or water symbols. Water is shown rippling, splashing, dripping, or falling and is the environment in which part or all of the action takes place on the majority of the stelae analyzed. Scroll-eyed heads and dragon heads symbolize water; the tree that has as its base a dragon head also bears fruit that is consumed by fish. Figures are seen fishing, feeding fish, sitting in boats, supported by or emerging from the mouth of a crocodile monster, diving into water, and being rained upon. Figures that perform duties over incense also seem to be directing their attention to water deities or animals and wear their symbols or attributes.

The analysis by Quirarte (1976: 77) of abstracted topline designs adds to the number of water references. Quirarte reports that these topline designs are references to a composite feline-serpentine creature. The diagonal bands on the body of the double-headed serpent that frames the scene on Stela 12 (Fig. 22b) are "definitely the markings on the body of this creature." Thus, the topline designs that refer to the jaguar and serpent are also references to water. Because the slanted U shape framed by diagonal bars appears on Stela 5 in lieu of the regular double-opposing diagonals (seen in other Izapa-style monuments), Quirarte (1976: 78, 84) also feels that the U element is a reference to a feline with serpent and saurian characteristics.

Second, the Izapa art style draws upon natural flora and fauna and animal behavior to give concrete expression to the idea of water. Jaguars (*Fe-*

lis onca), for example, spend much of their time in water and are adept swimmers (Perry 1970: 24–25). Natives of the area say that during a heavy rain is the best time to hunt jaguars. Another important creature in Izapa art is the water serpent that is frequently encountered in the area's streams. There are many fruit-bearing streamside trees as well, such as sapodilla (*Achras zapota*), marachan fan palm (*Sabal mexicana*), or the tomatillo. The fruit of the tomatillo is a favorite food of fish.[6] A small native crocodile (*Crocodylus acutus*) lives along the stream bank and spends much of its time in the water. Some native birds in the hawk family, such as the osprey, soar high in the air and dive suddenly and dramatically upon fish. The large size of these birds, with a huge wing span, makes their fishing activities all the more spectacular.

Flowing through the site of Izapa, from the highlands to the Pacific, is the small Rio Izapa. The amount of water in the river is greatly reduced during the dry season, and the appearance of water-dependent animals varies with the seasonal changes in rainfall. The concern for water on the part of the Izapa may have been heightened by the pronounced dry season. It is as likely, however, that the choice of water-related animals and vegetation as artistic symbols was made in conjunction with the formulation of religious beliefs and rituals. Such rituals somewhere had origins in pan-Mesoamerican belief systems. These original beliefs included symbolic representations of jaguars with serpent and bird characteristics, as seen in the designs from the Olmec area (Drucker 1952: 194). The results of this

analysis of Izapa visual traits and themes suggest, however, that the Izapa chose to reinterpret the older beliefs, selecting from them, developing, and adding to them characteristics that suited a belief system centered around water and water deities.

Quirarte (1973: 33) writes of the Izapa sculptors' propensity to abstract, and many but not all of the visual elements are expressed as abbreviated, complicated monsters or deities. A highly developed system of abstract symbols indicates a general common understanding of their meaning. When we try to look for stylistic periods in Izapa art, a consideration of the development from realism to abstraction may be useful. A cycle of abstraction to realism or its reverse may have in fact occurred at Izapa; there are no dates to confirm either trend. Whether or not the Izapa art style developed from or towards abstraction, however, the significance of the basic elements was well established and continuous. The crocodile monster, for instance, appears as highly realistic on Stela 25 (Fig. 39b) and as greatly abstracted on Stela 11 (Fig. 12a). Table 1 shows the repetition on separate stelae of groups of visual traits. It is these traits that are placed in the same context (cf. Kubler 1967: 12–13 and Panofsky 1960: 84) but changed in form that will provide the basis for future study of changes in the Izapa art style.

Classification and Interpretation: Izapa Stelae

Groups of associated visual traits determine Izapa iconography; these groups can also serve as a basis for the thematic clustering of the stelae. The stelae dendogram (Table 3, see also Table 1) shows how the stelae cluster when they are compared for shared visual traits. The various levels of similarity between clusters are indicated by the scale at the top and bottom of the dendogram; the specific coefficients for the most similar pairs of stelae are listed to the right. In interpreting the dendogram, seven clusters of stelae are chosen.

---

[6]The ramon (*Brosimum alicastrum*) has been of considerable interest as a possible, important, food source, beginning in the Preclassic, for the non-riverine Maya (Puleston n.d.; Puleston and Puleston 1971: 335–336; Lambert and Arnason 1982: 298–299). Norman (1976: 65, 195–196) identifies the tree on Izapa Stela 5 as a ramon. This "middle story" tree, however, is not characteristic of the Soconusco shore and coastal plain or of the transition to bocacosta forest near Tapachula, Chiapas (Shelford 1963: 425–427), and is not a likely candidate for representation in Izapa art. While the sapodilla (*Achras zapota*) is also a "middle story" tropical fruit tree, it does occur as the "upper story" of the better watered areas of the bocacosta, along with the deciduous *ceiba* (Coe and Flannery 1967: 11).

These groups are similar at a minimum level of 0.2000 and are indicated at the far right of the dendogram.[7]

The first cluster is comprised of Stelae 1 and 23 (Fig. 51). In general, water is the subject of these stelae, and an aqueous theme is expressed in a variety of ways. Water framed by opposing, scroll-eyed heads occurs at the base of both scenes (Trait Group 3); fish, and someone handling a serpent are shown on Stela 1. Each carving has as its focus a single large figure that is shown in profile or three-quarter view. Overlapping is also used in both scenes (Trait Groups 1 and 2). The fantastic attributes of the figure on Stela 1 and the superhuman action of the Stela 23 figure suggest that they portray deities. Both personages are placed in an aquatic environment, and the action clearly depends on the presence of water rather than merely coinciding with it. Stela 1 additionally depicts falling water along with fins and band-type bracelets (Trait Group 9), and falling water may be shown on Stela 23 although its depiction as vase-shaped differs from other examples. Stelae 1 and 23 are also similar in that their central figures wear serpentine loincloth ties. These ties are featured as an actual serpent on Stela 1 and as a bifurcated tongue on Stela 23. The loincloth tie on Stela 23 is shown with two other associated traits, the pose of falling or diving, and the picture plane divided into two regions vertically (Trait Group 5). A counterpart for the division of the picture plane on Stela 23 is the unique occurrence on Stela 1 of a scene above the topline design.

Stelae 6 and 26 (which is partially destroyed) form a second cluster (Fig. 52). These two stelae

are paired most specifically because they share traits associated with serpents (Trait Group 8). For example, the bifurcated tongue emerging from the mouth, the U-shaped element with a human head, and the action of holding something on the tongue or in the mouth are all traits that appear on Stela 6. On Stela 26, only the bifurcated tongues and the U element are visible. The more general features that compare on the two stelae are (from Trait Group 1) vertical perspective, a large seated figure, and the use of overlapping.

Stelae 6 and 26 also share other related traits. The figure on Stela 6 wears band-type anklets and bracelets, and falling water is represented behind this creature (Trait Group 9). The jewelry type cannot be determined on Stela 26, but falling water (in a form nearly identical to that on Stela 6) is shown to the far right, and a mountain glyph appears at the bottom of the scene. Crocodile feet also occur on Stela 6 (Trait Group 5), but the traits usually associated with these appendages are not present. (The serpent tail of the beast compares to, but is not the equivalent of, the bifurcated tongue in the same context.) The crocodile feet are a reference to water, the overall theme of both of these carvings. The items emphasized on these two stelae are falling water (as well as water at the top of the scene on Stela 26), serpent or reptilian attributes (especially bifurcated tongues), and the canoe-shaped U element.

Stelae 8, 10, and 27 form the third group of thematically related stelae (Fig. 53). Each stela has a seated figure shown in profile, and overlapping is employed to some extent. Also, Stelae 10 and 27 have standing figures that are fractionally represented, and figures on all of the stelae are placed on a groundline (Trait Groups 1 and 2). A highly associated pair of traits, the illusion of recession and the Kan Cross cartouche appear on Stelae 8 and 27; in each case a figure is enclosed by the glyph.

In this group of stelae, water is suggested primarily by animals that are associated with aqueous themes (Trait Groups 5, 10, and 11). For instance, on Stela 27 a small winged figure dives

[7]There are several reasons why this dendogram does not show higher levels of similarity between stelae. First, there are data missing because some stelae are broken or eroded. Second, these relationships are determined by the visual traits, or the content, rather than by stylistic considerations, or the way in which individual forms are handled. Not accounted for, then, are the qualities of a realistic or abstract presentation of the same subject; these characteristics may reflect chronological differences. Third, the main point of the stelae dendogram is that it supports and adds to the interpretation of the visual traits.

or falls within the cartouche (Trait Group 5), and a tree-dragon appears on Stelae 10 and 27 (Trait Group 10). Stela 8 may also show a kind of dragon; the creature is suggested by the curved long toes of the monster and the head-shaped scrollwork to the right of the cartouche. (The upper portion of this stela is too damaged to determine its design for certain. The feet of the possible dragon may be those of a jaguar instead.) The tree-dragon is shown with heart-shaped leaves on Stela 10 (Trait Group 10), while on Stela 27 the dragon head is found alongside palm or paddle-shaped leaves (Trait Group 11). There is yet another dragon on Stela 27 below the groundline upon which the figures stand. Further, on this stela the fruit of the tree-dragon is given to a jaguar. Conspicuously absent on all of these stelae are any traits that illustrate or refer to serpents. Water is implied by the presence of the dragon, the jaguar, and/or the diving figure, but no specific example of water is shown.

Stelae 14, 18, and 24 form the next group of related stelae (Fig. 54). Although Stelae 14 and 24 are badly damaged and much information is missing, this group is nevertheless distinguished by portraying the least action of all the Izapa stelae. The expression emphasized seems to be ceremonial and comparatively solemn. For instance, on each of the three stelae there is at least one pair of seated, opposing profile figures. These figures attend incense burners on Stelae 18 and 24, and it is possible that an incense burner was present on Stela 14 as well. The attendants on Stelae 18 and 24 are further dignified by wearing necklaces of rounded beads (Trait Group 4). Since all of the compositions appear to be symmetrical, the formality of the occasion portrayed is accentuated (Trait Group 2).

The seated figures on Stelae 18 and 24 are placed on a groundline and some overlapping (though to a small degree) is employed (Trait Group 1). It is altogether possible that these figures who gesture over incense burners anticipate action by deities. Such a deity may be represented on Stela 24, judging by the large size of the ele-

vated central figure. Unfortunately the broken and missing upper portion of this stela limits analysis. Possibly the area was filled with a double-headed sky serpent as shown on Stela 18. Another likely motif could be a jaguar. This suggestion is supported by the placement of the feline on Stela 14 (and on Stela 12 in Stela Group 6). Since both serpents and jaguars are associated with water, either motif might have been represented. Thus, water would have figured importantly in the ceremony depicted. Furthermore, the jaguar-associated hill glyph may be seen only on Stela 14; Norman (1976: 48) interprets this glyph as a "jaguar snout" water motif.

Momentarily passing over the fifth group of stelae, Stela Group 6, comprised of Stelae 5, 12, and 25, (Fig. 56) is discussed next because this group shares important characteristics with Stela Group 4. An example is a seated pair of figures on Stela 5 who attend an incense burner identical to that shown on Stela 24 (Trait Group 4). Stelae 5 and 18 are related to Stela 24 in that there are attendants behind the persons who gesture over incense. On Stela 5 one of these persons holds an umbrella and the other an instrument that might be a musical rasp. Additionally, the smoke that is emitted from all of the illustrated incense burners is similar. Another relationship between Stela Group 6 and Stela Group 4 is the placement of the two seated figures beneath the jaguar on Stela 12, a more elaborate version of the scene from Stela 14.

In direct contrast to the solemnity of Stela Group 4, however, Stelae 5, 12, and 25 are extremely narrative; scenes of violent action, including blood, are represented on Stelae 12 and 25. For instance on Stela 12 blood flows from the mouth of the jaguar, and on Stela 25 the amputated arm of the standing figure bleeds profusely. Stela 5 shows every kind of gesture including (from Trait Group 7) a figure wearing a cloak and carrying a small person on his back.

All three of these stelae from Group VI share with the third group of stelae (Stelae 8, 10, and 27) the depiction of a tree-dragon and/or a jaguar. Specifically, a realistic crocodile metamorphoses into a tree with heart-shaped leaves on Stela 25. Two birds are also shown (Trait Group 10). A tree with heart-shaped leaves ascends from a dragon-head base on Stela 5 where a water bird perches on one branch of the tree and two of the figures standing nearby are duck-billed. Fruit also appears on this tree (Trait Group 11). On Stela 12, a tree is formed by branches supported by a double-headed serpent. Again, the leaves on the branches are heart-shaped, and while this tree has no dragon origins, a netted jaguar is suspended from its branches.

Stelae 5 and 12 share several additional traits: the double-headed earth serpent, band-type anklets or bracelets, the mountain and jaguar glyphs, and falling water (Trait Group 9). Water is suggested on Stela 25 by the unique representation of a conch shell on the crocodile's nose, and although serpents are represented on all of the three stelae, the one on Stela 25 does not have two heads. These stelae also share the portrayal of profile or three-quarter view figures (Trait Group 2) as well as the use of a groundline (Trait Group 1). Overlapping occurs, too, and vertical perspective is shown on Stelae 5 and 25 (Trait Group 1).

To return to Stela Group 5 (Fig. 55), it is large, and includes Stelae 2, 3, 4, 7, 11, 21, and 60. Within this group, the badly damaged Stelae 7 and 60 are somewhat set apart from the other related works. Shown on both stelae is a pair of figures posed so that one figure stands and bends over his counterpart. These figures may be connected with the ball game if their knee-pads bear such an association. (The figure on Stela 3 wears knee-pads as well, but the opponent is non-human.) The action depicted is unclear, but either the standing figure simply supports the seated figure, or he removes something from him—perhaps an insignia or even a vital organ.

The other characteristics of Stelae 7 and 60 can be compared in a discussion of the rest of the stelae in Group 5. Stelae 2, 4, 11, and 60 share several related traits: a falling or diving figure who wears wings, bifurcated-tongue loincloth ties, crocodile feet, and the picture ground divided into upper and lower regions (Trait Group 5). All of these motifs are seen on Stela 2; on Stela 4 the feet of the diving figure are possibly crocodilian rather than avian or human. The bifurcated-tongue belt does not occur on Stela 11, but its placement would have been obscured by the monster. Also, this stela's winged figure does not fall or dive. The action of falling or diving is represented differently on Stela 60. Here, the avian has already fallen and lies crumpled at the base of the scene. Above, the standing figure probably wears a bifurcated-tongue belt tie (incomplete in its present condition). The use of picture ground cannot be determined, though, because of the damage to the stela.

Dragons are suggested by the use of crocodilian feet, but they are represented in other ways on these stelae. The tree-dragon (Trait Group 10), for instance, is shown on Stela 2 where the falling figure wears a dragon headdress. (Traits related to the dragon head, the palm-shaped tree leaves and fruit—all in Trait Group 11—also appear on Stela 2.) The tree-dragon is not represented on Stela 11, but a crocodile monster crouches at the base of the scene and supports the winged figure above or in his mouth.

Serpents are also part of the subject matter of this stelae group. Double-headed earth serpents occur on Stelae 7 and 11 (Trait Group 9). The serpent's tongue is also shown along with the action of holding something on or in the mouth, and the canoe-shaped U element (Trait Group 8). On Stela 3, for example, the glyph is balanced on the tongue of the serpent. Also occurring on this stela are the action of fighting a serpent, a single-headed snake, and a scroll-eyed head (Trait Group 3).

Nearly all of the Group 5 stelae (with the exception of Stela 7) present the largest figures in fractionally represented poses (Trait Group 1). These works are clearly organized by such formally posed figures who are often armed and shown in the context of avian and saurian elements. Consequently the most common actions portrayed are beheading, and falling or diving.

The final group of thematically related stelae is comprised of Stelae 9, 22, 50, and 67 (Fig. 57). In particular, Stelae 22, 50, and 67 are united by traits that have been shown to be related to water (Trait Group 3). For instance, on Stelae 22 and 50 a serpent is held or wrestled and a serpentine form winds upward and outward from the central figure on Stela 67. Scroll-eyed heads also occur on Stelae 22 and 50 (and probably were present on Stela 67 as well if the inference can be made from the overall similarities of this carving to Stela 22). Additionally, Stelae 22 and 67 share opposing bodiless heads, fish, and water at the base of the scene.

Further associating Stelae 9, 22, and 67 are their symmetrical compositions (Trait Group 3). Stela 9 also shares with Stela 50 the use of vertical perspective (Trait Group 1). These two stelae are unique in their representation of figures wearing stiff cloaks (Trait Group 7). Other traits associated with vertical perspective—standing figures, large figures, figures placed on a groundline, overlapping, seated individuals, and fractional representation—occur in varying combinations on all four stelae in Group 7.

The clusters formed by the related stelae show that particular stelae share common themes. To go beyond this point to try to recognize relationships between themes, or co-occurring clusters of traits, it is necessary to rely on more subjective explanations and interpretations. These interpretations are based on visual evidence of the formal and iconographic relationships between the themes presented together on each stela.

When the groups of stelae are reviewed with regard to the clustering of trait groups, both pairing and division occur. For example, Trait Group 3 may occur with Trait Group 5, thus combining the scroll-eyed head, water, and serpent motifs with the falling or diving winged figure. Alternatively, Trait Group 3 motifs may occur with the glyphs, serpent, and water characteristics of Trait Group 9. In yet another combination, traits associated with the dragon from Trait Groups 9 and 10 are combined with Trait Group 5. Trait

Group 4, emphasizing incense burners, occurs alone or with the dragon- and tree-oriented Trait Groups 10 and 11. In one group of stelae the beheading pose and a weapon from Trait Group 6 are juxtaposed with Trait Groups 5, 10, and 11. Also, the canoe-shaped U element, the gesture of holding something on the tongue or in the mouth, and the bifurcated tongue from Trait Group 8, sometimes occur with Trait Group 9. Trait Group 9 is large and includes six visual traits that are concerned with water or serpents. While half of this trait group occurs with Trait Groups 3 and 8, the entire trait group is represented alongside Trait Groups 4, 10, and 11. Trait Group 7—the cloak, baton, and the action of carrying a small person—occurs alone when all three traits are present, or with Trait Groups 3, 9, 10, and 11 where it is represented by two traits only.

Clearly, the themes on the stelae are related. The dominant themes are: scroll-eyed heads, serpents, and a water environment (Trait Group 3); the falling or diving figure with saurian characteristics (Trait Group 5); the weapon-holding figure posed as if to behead (Trait Group 6); and the dragon-tree combination (Trait Groups 10, 11). A secondary theme is the canoe-shaped U element combined with the action of holding something in the mouth (Trait Group 8). Finally, the water-related dragon and serpent themes of the other trait groups are reinforced by the clustering of the mountain and jaguar glyphs, the earth serpent, and other water references (Trait Group 9).

Interpretation: Religion

It has been established that there is an Izapa iconography, but does this iconography reflect an Izapa religion? While deliberately avoiding overstressing the relationship between iconography and religion, some interpretations can be offered here. Rappaport (1971), divides the operation of religions into three categories: "ultimate sacred propositions," ritual, and religious experience. Perhaps the kinds of ultimate sacred propositions, or completely unverifiable beliefs, that are held as unquestionable truths by the faithful (Rappaport 1971: 29) and that were part of reality for the Izapa, are modifications of a Mesoamerican primeval origin myth. A reconstruction of this myth, derived from Maya codices and iconography as well as Aztec cosmology, can be summarized as follows:

Hunab, or Hunab Ku, was the creator of the world we know and three before it. Each previous creation was destroyed by deluge.

The creator Hunab was the father-mother of Itzamna whose duty it was to rule all other deities. Itzamna was thus lord of the heavens, and of day and night. (The invention of writing and books is attributed to this god who is represented in the codices as an old man with toothless jaws and sunken cheeks.)

Among the gods ruled by Itzamna were the four Bacabs. The Bacabs were brothers whom Hunab placed at the four points of the world to hold up the sky and to prevent its collapse. In the Mexican myths, this role was given to four Tezcatlepocas who created the four world trees to help in the great task. The Bacabs escaped the great flood.

The Bacabs were closely associated with Chac, the long-nosed god of rain. Benevolent Chac existed as the four gods of the cardinal points. He is associated with, or perhaps is the same as, the wind god.

Itzamna also ruled Ah Puch, the skeletal god of death. Ah Puch presided as chief demon over the lowest of the nine Maya underworlds.

In the Maya view, the earth was the lowest of thirteen layered heavens. Below the earth were nine underworlds, also superimposed. After death, worthy people were believed to journey to a paradise where there grew a great *yaxche* or sacred ceiba tree. Eternal rest and comfort were offered in the shade of this tree. The less fortunate Maya were doomed to torment in the bottom-most hell.

The tension between the upper and lower worlds is a theme throughout Mayan mythology. In the earliest days of creation the gods of the underworld seized those of the heavens. In the process, the great serpent of the heavens was taken away, the sky fell, and the earth was flooded. When the Bacabs ordained the creation of a new world, they caused four great trees to rise. As symbols of the destruction beneath, a bird was to perch in the yellow and black trees. Last to rise was a green tree of abundance in the center of the world.

The references to the world consisting of water, the death, water, and wind gods, trees suporting the sky, and the sky serpent are all more or less consistent with Izapa iconography. The particular Izapa interpretation or version of the myth, nevertheless, must remain their own. For instance, a bird does perch on the branches of the crocodile-tree on Stela 25, and a duck or pelican appears in the upper right of Stela 5. There are no truly obvious representatives of a ceiba, however. Also, some trees (Stelae 5 and 27) contact the celestial panel and thus support the "sky" (Norman 1976: 65), while others (Stelae 2 and 25) do not. Two of the trees (Stelae 2 and 27) have four branches, possibly corresponding to the four directional parts of the world in later Maya conceptions (Norman 1976: 66–67), but two other trees (Stelae 5 and 25) have five and eight divisions, respectively. While it is possible to identify many elements of Maya and Mexican mythology in Izapa art (especially in Stela 5, analyzed so thoroughly by Norman [1976: 165–236]), superimposing a Postclassic framework has many risks. On the other hand, the consistent rendering of water, and lowland flora and fauna on Izapa monuments provides excellent data for future etiological and ecological studies.[8]

Religious ritual on the part of the Izapa most likely took place in anticipation of the rainy season. The dramatic narrative scenes literally or symbolically emphasize water. Specifically, these rituals may have included head-taking, the offering of incense, and perhaps child sacrifice (where a large figure carries a smaller one, as on Stelae 5 and 9).

However, wider interpretations of religious behavior are less identifiable at this time. Functions of this behavior, such as the regulation of man-land ratios or the redistribution of goods, have not been determined. Some headway has been

[8]T. Dillehay and P. Kaulicke (n.d.) use this method to examine the question of why certain plants and animals were selected as essential design motifs in Precolumbian art. Specifically, carnivorous felines, eagles, snakes, and crocodiles are dominant themes. The choice of these animals represents their cognitive significance in the human mind and is linked to human socio-spatial organization. Further, these authors propose that the selective process is most intense in Late Formative cultures and in the context of a tropical forest or adjacent environment.

made, though, by Stocker et al. (1980) who propose a model for Olmec-highlands trade that is centered on crocodiles and crocodilian iconography. After demonstrating that the Olmec crocodile is at least as important as the jaguar as a water, vegetation, fertility, and abundance symbol, these researchers examine the animal's role in trade. They suggest that "less sophisticated highland elites may have been willing to trade their exotic raw materials (hematite, jade, etc.) and the obsidian that was imperative for tools in return, at least in part, for the crocodilian, the embodiment of the Olmec's successful ideology bonding crocodilian to rain, corn, and earth fertility" (Stocker et al. 1980: 749).

Whether or not the crocodile in Izapa art is a manifestation of the Maya Itzam Na (Thompson 1970: 216–218), its importance in Izapa iconography as a water-fertility symbol cannot be denied. As in the case of the Olmec, Izapa iconography reflects a lowland riverine environment by its representation of specific animals and plants. Crocodiles may have been important as a preagricultural food source and export item in Izapa history, and an ecological explanation of their deification may eventually shed light on their economic and religious affiliations with other sites.

Classification and Interpretation: Comparison of Izapa Stelae to Works from Related Sites

One focus of this study has been to determine if the stelae and carvings from other sites are indeed examples of the Izapa art style. Among the sites most frequently included in studies of Izapa art are Abaj Takalik, Kaminaljuyu, El Baul, Bilbao, Chiapa de Corzo, and El Jobo. In order to be considered "Izapa," works from these sites must share the visual traits of the Izapa stelae. More importantly, however, the visual traits must be organized in a similar manner.

The most frequently labelled "Izapa" stelae are: Kaminaljuyu Stelae 4, 10, 11, and 19; Abaj Taka-

lik Stelae 1, 2, 3, and 5; El Baul Stela 1 (Herrera Stela); Bilbao Monument 42; El Jobo Stela 1, and Chiapa de Corzo Bone Carving 1. To determine if these stelae are Izapa in style, they were first examined for Izapa visual traits. Together, these twelve works contain only twenty-nine of the fifty-four identified Izapa visual traits (Tables 4, 5). In addition, six distinctive traits which do *not* occur at Izapa appear on these stelae from other sites (Table 6).

Of the traits that do not occur at Izapa, the first two relate to clothing. A kilt or tripart belt (CKILT) is worn by the figures on Abaj Takalik Stela 5 and Bilbao Monument 42 (Figs. 44, 40e). The belt or belt ornament is very similar to the lower part of the belt-head illustrated by Proskouriakoff (1950: Fig. 23 E1) as a Classic Maya element. Also foreign to Izapa is the knotted anklet (CKNTA) worn by figures on Abaj Takalik Stelae 1 and 5 (Figs. 43a, 44), El Jobo Stela 1 (Fig. 41a), and Kaminaljuyu Stela 11 (Fig. 41b). The knotted anklet may be compared to Proskouriakoff's example of the Early Classic simple knotted anklet from Stela 10 at Uaxactun (1950: Fig. 28 G1).

A third visual trait that does not occur at Izapa but that occurs on Abaj Takalik Stelae 1, 2, and 5 (Figs. 43a, 45a, 44), and El Baul Stela 1 (Fig. 43b), is the use of vertically aligned inscriptions (THIER). Hieroglyphs that are vertically arranged also appear on Kaminaljuyu Stela 10 (Fig. 42). According to Graham (1977: 196), "the Maya monuments at Abaj Takalik carry hieroglyphic inscriptions in a very early form of Maya writing. The recently discovered Stela 5, for instance, has two early Maya Initial Series dates, the later of which corresponds to A.D. 126." The date on El Baul Stela 1, at A.D. 11 (Graham et al. 1978: 91 [new reading by Graham]), places it chronologically between Abaj Takalik Stela 5 and Abaj Takalik Stela 2 which Graham (1977: 197) has reread as "probably no later than 1st Century B.C." Columns of hieroglyphs occur regularly on Classic Maya stelae.

A fourth trait that does not occur at Izapa is

also characteristic of Classic Maya art. This trait is the act of holding one or both arms against the body, with fingers curled outward towards the shoulder (DHDCS). The Maya figures often hold a serpent bar (as illustrated by Proskouriakoff 1950: Fig. 31 B1, B2). This pose occurs at Abaj Takalik on Stelae 1 and 5 (Figs. 43a, 44).

The use of multiple levels of carving away the surface of the stela to define the figure and details of the figure (SMULT) is an artistic device not employed by Izapa sculptors. Where the Izapa relied most often upon incised lines and overlapping to define figures, the carvers of Kaminaljuyu Stela 11 (Fig. 41b) and Kaminaljuyu Stela 10 (Fig. 42) relied upon carving away their designs in three or more levels starting from the original surface of the stone. It might also be mentioned here that the carving techniques utilized for both the Izapa and the Kaminaljuyu stelae contrast sharply with the Olmec practice of carving the surface of the stone with modelled forms that are defined by rounded contours. The modelling of the Olmec works gives a three-dimensional quality that is lacking in the more surface-oriented Izapa and Kaminaljuyu carvings.

Yet another trait that occurs on Kaminaljuyu Stelae 10 and 11 (Figs. 42, 41b) is a tripart club with a curved object (probably a flint axe) attached. This weapon is held in the left hand of the standing figure on Kaminaljuyu Stela 10. Proskouriakoff illustrates a similar hatchet from Xcalumkim, South Building of the Glyphic Group (Proskouriakoff 1950: Fig. 34 T2y), and reports that hatchets were rarely represented in Classic Maya carving (1950: 98).

While these first four traits that occur on stelae outside the site of Izapa are characteristic of Maya art, the Izapa stelae do not bear traits clearly related to the Classic Maya art style. Proskouriakoff (1950: 177), however, points out some Izapa traits similar to the Early Period. For example, there is an "early type of plume indication which uses overlapping planes and a line near one edge of each feather" on Izapa Stela 4; yet she finds it difficult to judge whether the peculiarities of Stela

4 are due to a period of independent invention or are the result of local taste.

Another trait that is shared by Izapa stelae and those from other sites is the downward-peering head (HDNPR). Downward-peering heads occurr only twice at Izapa, on Stela 4 (Fig. 15b) (where the trait is the head of the falling figure) and on Stela 7 (Fig. 15c). A downward-peering head is shown on Kaminaljuyu Stela 11 (Fig. 41b), at Tikal on Stelae 29 (Fig. 45b) and 4 (Miles 1965: Fig. 9d), on El Baul Stela 1 (Fig. 43b), and at Abaj Takalik on Stela 2 (Fig. 45a). Further, a downward-peering figure appears on Stela D, Tres Zapotes (Fig. 50).

Outside of the fact that all of these heads are downward-peering, the renderings are very different. For example, the downward-peering head on Izapa Stela 7 has the typical Izapa two-part earplug as does the head referred to on Izapa Stela 4. These heads are not surrounded by profuse scrollwork as they are on the Abaj Takalik and El Baul stelae where the earplugs are of a different type as well. On the Abaj Takalik and El Baul stelae, the heads are clearly human; at Izapa the faces are not visible due to damage. The head on Kaminaljuyu Stela 11 is not human at all but a form of a dragon. Also, this head is made nearly unrecognizable by the many overpowering details such as U elements and double outlining of the forms. Alternately, the downward-peering head on Tikal Stela 29 (Fig. 45b) is a masked human, and the headdress is made of elements not found on the other stelae. Furthermore, Tikal Stela 29 has no other connection to the Izapa art style; no other "Izapa" traits are present. In fact, the hand curved inward and holding an early type of serpent bar is a Maya characteristic found at Abaj Takalik. Finally, the head on Tikal Stela 4 is similar only to. that on Tikal Stela 29, and then only by weak similarities between the earplugs.

Downward-peering heads, then, are not a specifically Izapa characteristic, although Izapa rendering differs from rendering at related sites. The wide distribution in space of these downward-peering heads, as well as the differences in their rendering, suggests that this trait was popular and widespread during the Late Preclassic and Early Classic; however, this trait cannot be said to have originated at Izapa or to be a specifically Izapa visual trait.

Of the remaining twenty-eight visual traits shared by the Izapa stelae and the stelae from outside sites that are frequently *called* "Izapa," at least fourteen characteristics can and do occur virtually anywhere in Mesoamerican art. These traits are: the standing figure, a large figure, a seated individual, a figure shown in profile, small figures, fractional representation, knee-pads, a cloak, a curved staff or baton, jaguars, serpents, posing as if to behead someone, symmetrical composition, and shallow spatial depth. These traits are not significant by their presence at Izapa alone or anywhere else. They gain significance by the context in which they appear.

Fourteen of the twenty-nine shared visual traits are more typically Izapa due to their frequent occurrence on Izapa stelae (see Table 5). They are: space divided into upper and lower regions, a band-type anklet or bracelet, the dragon head, scroll-eyed heads, fins, crocodile feet, falling water, wings, the pose of holding or wrestling a serpent, bifurcated-tongue loincloth ties, serpent appendages, heart-shaped tree leaves, incense burners, an extensive use of overlapping, and vertical perspective. The presence of these visual traits on stelae from other sites indicates some relationship with Izapa; if these traits appear in the same groups or context as they do at Izapa, there is also strong evidence for the presence of the Izapa style.

Each of the stelae from sites outside Izapa are now examined to determine the degree of their relationship to Izapa. We begin with Kaminaljuyu Stelae 4, 10, 11, and 19 which are cited by Quirarte (1973: 34) and Miles (1965: 242–264), among others, as closely related to Izapa-style art. Kaminaljuyu Stela 11 (Fig. 41b) bears twelve traits found on the Izapa stelae. They are: a standing figure, a large figure, fractional representation, a crooked or curved staff, a downward-peering head, shallow spatial depth with the figure standing on a groundline, the dragon head, a stiff cloak, a bilaterally symmetrical composition, a bifurcated-tongue loincloth tie, incense burners, and heart-shaped tree leaves. There is also use of the Izapa baseline motif. This substantial number of Izapa traits undoubtedly reflects an influence from Izapa art at Kaminaljuyu. The apparent influence, however, is one of form rather than meaning. For instance, the downward-peering head, and the stiff cloak worn by the Kaminaljuyu figure, are traits that appear together on Tres Zapotes Stela D (Fig. 50), but not on the Izapa stelae. The large standing figure that is fractionally represented and shown standing on a groundline corresponds to the Izapa arrangement of visual elements (Trait Group 1); however, the co-occurrence of a crooked staff and the stiff cloak (Trait Group 7) demonstrates an Olmec influence at Kaminaljuyu as much as it shows a relationship to Izapa. There are two incense burners shown on this stela, but they are not attended by a pair of (or individual) seated figures (Trait Group 4). Also, the bifurcated-tongue loincloth tie does not appear with any other traits in Trait Group 5. Only if we accept Quirarte's (1976: 84) interpretation of the downward-peering head on the Kaminaljuyu stela as an abbreviated winged figure is there a connection at all to the Izapa trait group. Quirarte's interpretation may be quite correct—the dragon head on the Kaminaljuyu stela does correspond to the dragon head on the downward-falling figure on Izapa Stela 2 and the headdress on the winged standing figure on Izapa Stela 4. Further, the dragon-head motif belongs with Trait Group 11, a cluster related to Trait Group 10, where a dragon-tree and heart-shaped tree leaves are featured. While the dragon head on Kaminaljuyu Stela 11 is not associated with a tree at all, the heart-shaped tree leaf does occur as part of the headdress of the standing figure. The standing figure on Izapa Stela 25 also has a leaf headdress, but he appears with a tree-dragon.

Finally, Kaminaljuyu Stela 11 has three traits that do not occur at Izapa: the use of multiple levels of surface carving, the knotted anklet, and the distinctive obsidian axe or flint weapon. All Izapa figures shown holding a knife or a club are posed as if to behead, a direct contrast with the Kaminaljuyu stela. While this stela bears some similarities to Izapa content as well as form, then, it also has some major differences. Judging by similarities between Kaminaljuyu Stela 11 and the Izapa stelae, the Kaminaljuyu stela, designated as Miraflores by Shook (Heath-Jones: 1959), was probably carved when the sites were in regular contact and were borrowing visual traits. The differences between this stela and the Izapa examples indicate that, at the time the stelae were carved, Izapa and Kaminaljuyu maintained distinct artistic identities.

Kaminaljuyu Stela 10 (Fig. 42) shares only seven visual traits with the Izapa stelae. There are two large, standing figures. One figure, fractionally represented, wears winglike appendages or a back panel, and is posed as if to behead; another figure is shown in profile. Also, the dragon head appears as a small element of the headdress of the figure posed as if to behead. Further, Kaminaljuyu Stela 10 has three traits that do not occur on the Izapa stelae: vertically arranged hieroglyphs, the use of multiple levels of carving, and the axe or weapon with a flint. The combined characteristics of the large, standing figure that is fractionally represented agrees with Izapa Trait Group 1. The placement of this figure in the picture space may indicate that vertical perspective was used as well, although the lower part of the stela is destroyed. There is no symmetrical composition, however, and the co-occurrence of two very large figures, one fractionally represented and one shown in profile, is not in keeping with the Izapa format, particularly where the gesture of beheading is featured. The Izapa trait of wings, or wearing a winglike costume, is specified by Trait Group 5 to co-occur with falling or diving figures and reptilian or serpentine characteristics. None of these traits is present on Kaminaljuyu Stela 10. While at Izapa the figure posed as if to behead may occur with a downward-peering

head (Trait Group 6) as it does on Izapa Stela 4 (and there the downward-peering head is the head of a diving figure), the Kaminaljuyu stela has no downward-peering head. Instead, it shows a large, possibly disembodied, fanged, and elaborately decorated head, right-side up. The dragon head is merely a small element of an elaborate headdress on the Kaminaljuyu stela; at Izapa the dragon head is always large—when shown in the context of a headdress, it is the entire headdress.

Kaminaljuyu Stela 10 is even less similar to the Izapa stelae than Kaminaljuyu Stela 11. Overall, this stela is a poor candidate for inclusion in the Izapa art style. On Kaminaljuyu Stela 10 there are clearly Maya hieroglyphs that appear in conjunction with Maya detail and the use of Izapa visual traits in a way not consistent with the Izapa stelae.

Contrasting with Kaminaljuyu Stelae 10 and 11, Kaminaljuyu Stelae 4 (Fig. 40c) and 19 (Fig. 40d) bear none of the six traits that are found only on stelae from outside the site of Izapa. Additionally, these two stelae do portray fourteen traits found on Izapa stelae. First, Kaminaljuyu Stelae 4 and 19 both have a large figure with crocodile feet, fins, and serpent appendages and are shown in vertical perspective; both works also have a scroll-eyed head, falling water, and utilize overlapping forms. Furthermore, the figure on Kaminaljuyu Stela 19 is kneeling, fractionally represented, and presented in a symmetrical composition. He holds a serpent that has a snake's head and a scroll-eyed head at the "tail." The figure also wears kneepads. The representation of a large seated figure shown in vertical perspective, fractionally represented, and with use of overlapping, agrees with Izapa Trait Group 1. Still, the basic symmetry of the composition does not agree with Trait Group 2 because there are no small or profile figures.

Kaminaljuyu Stela 19 has three traits from Trait Group 3: a scroll-eyed head, a serpent, and the act of holding or wrestling the serpent. There are no fish or opposing bodiless heads, but a connection to water is made by the representation of two traits from Group 9—falling water and fins. Serpent appendages and knee-pads are also a pair of correlated Izapa traits. The reptilian feet of the figure, however, appear without any other traits from Trait Group 5 where bird, serpent, and saurian elements are combined. Of the fourteen traits Kaminaljuyu Stela 19 shares with the Izapa stelae, only the context of crocodile feet and the use of symmetry fail to agree with the Izapa rules for design. Further, this stela emphasizes, in general, a water theme and portrays dramatic action; it can be said to be Izapa in style.

Kaminaljuyu Stela 4 shares at least nine visual traits with the Izapa stelae. Although the upper portion of this stela is missing, its semblance to Kaminaljuyu Stela 19 allows inference of some missing traits, such as holding a serpent. In addition, the centrally placed figure with crocodile feet has fins, wears knotted serpents, and is very similar on the two stelae. Only the pose of the figure, shown frontally on Stela 4, differs significantly. The scroll-eyed head, with scrollwork water tumbling beneath it, is comparably placed on both stelae. From these comparisons it is possible to say that the figure on Kaminaljuyu Stela 4 was also holding a serpent. The frontal pose, with both legs flattened outward, may indicate that the figure was fractionally represented. The large standing figure in vertical perspective, rendered with the technique of overlapping, agrees with Izapa Trait Group 1.

If the figure is indeed wrestling a serpent that has a scroll-eyed head as the tail, three traits from Trait Group 3 are present as well. Fins and falling water are traits that co-occur in Trait Group 6, and the figure wears knee-pads (although one is on the inside of the leg) that appear with the use of a serpent as an appendage or part of clothing on the Izapa stelae. As on Kaminaljuyu Stela 19, only the crocodile feet appear, without any other traits from the group in which this motif belongs. Kaminaljuyu Stela 4 may be compared to Izapa Stela 1 where the scroll-eyed head also occurs in falling water, and the round, tight scrolls are nearly identical. Furthermore, the figure on Izapa Stela 1 has a serpent's head loincloth tie or belt. Kaminaljuyu Stela 4 emphasizes the theme of water, and because it shares co-occurring traits with the Izapa groups of visual elements, it may be designated Izapa in style.

Next, El Jobo Stela 1 (Fig. 41a) also shares ten traits with the Izapa stelae: the large standing figure, a small profile figure, fractional representation, placement of the figure on a groundline, knee-pads, and a stave or staff. Only one shared visual trait, the scroll-eyed head, is specifically Izapa. In addition, the large El Jobo figure holds a decapitated head in his left hand so that the theme of beheading—though not the typical Izapa pose—is represented.

How do these traits compare to the Izapa trait groups? There is initial agreement in the large, fractionally represented figure shown standing on a groundline and thus matching Trait Group 1. However, there is little evidence of the use of overlapping here; the small figure is clearly separated from the larger one. The small figure presented in profile does agree with Izapa Trait Group 2, but the scene is not symmetrical. The large figure wears knee-pads (or has very wrinkled knees), although he does not have crocodile feet. His knotted anklets are not found on Izapa stelae. Further, a scroll-eyed head is present, yet it appears with no other traits in Trait Group 3. Conspicuously absent are any references, other than the scroll-eyed head, to water. The figure carries a staff or baton made of bone, and is unlike the Izapa counterparts on Izapa Stelae 9 and 10. The figure apparently does not wear a stiff cloak or carry a small person either; ordinarily these two traits co-occur with the staff or stave. Thus, while El Jobo is located very near Izapa, and Stela 1 from the site shares visual traits with the Izapa stelae (including an Izapa topline design), stylistically El Jobo Stela 1 cannot be clearly labelled Izapa.

El Baul Stela 1 (Fig. 43b) is another work that should be considered in this discussion. This stela has nine traits that are found on the Izapa stelae.

For instance, there is a large figure, fractionally represented, standing on a groundline. This figure also wears band-type anklets and holds a staff or baton of some kind in his right hand. Because the downward-peering head above the figure occupies a fairly large zone, the picture ground may be considered as divided into upper and lower regions. Also, behind the figure is a scroll-eyed head. Falling water may be indicated as well; the design on the topmost portion of the El Baul stela is similar not only to the rain (or water) glyph shown on the far right of Izapa Stela 12 (Fig. 36b), but also to the water-connected design on Sides C and D of Monument C, Tres Zapotes (Fig. 36a). El Baul Stela 1 might have an Izapa baseline design, too. This stela has one important non-Izapa trait, however—the vertically arranged hieroglyphs.

The visual traits on the El Baul stela do not compare well to the Izapa trait groups. While Trait Group 1 is represented in that the large standing figure stands on a groundline and is fractionally represented, overlapping is not employed. Additionally, the figure carries a baton but does not wear a cloak or carry a small child. The downward-peering head shown on El Baul Stela 1 does not co-occur with two other traits found in Izapa Trait Group 6: a knife or club, and a figure posed as if to behead someone. Furthermore, the scroll-eyed head appears on the El Baul stela without a single other trait from Trait Group 3; the same is true of the space divided into upper and lower regions—none of the other traits in Group 5 is present. Band-type anklets may be represented on this stela, and if the topmost design may be interpreted as falling water, two of the six traits from Trait Group 9 are present. While El Baul Stela 1 has some agreement with the Izapa stelae in the arrangement of visual traits, these agreements are not strong enough to insure that the monument is Izapa in style. Taking into consideration that nearly half of the composition of the stela is filled with hieroglyphs, any argument for the El Baul stela as an example of the Izapa art style is further weakened. Graham has also analyzed this stela and

agrees that is not only *not* Izapa, but fundamentally Maya (Graham et al. 1978: 98). It is unfortunate that there is no clear relationship between this stela and those from Izapa, since it is one of the few dated works that might have been useful in determining chronology.

Stelae 1, 2, 3, and 5 from Abaj Takalik (Figs. 43a, 45a, 43c, and 44) have a very limited share of Izapa visual traits. For example, Abaj Takalik Stela 1 has a large, fractionally represented figure that stands on a groundline. This figure wears a stylized serpent loincloth tie that may be considered similar to the use of a serpent as a belt or appendage on Izapa Stela 1. On the Abaj Takalik stela, though, the serpent loincloth has a dragon head at the end and a small jaguar perched on the tie's upper curve. While the idea of a serpent loincloth tie is Izapa, the representation of the idea here is totally unlike the Izapa examples. On the Izapa stelae, the jaguar and the serpent appendages are traits not found together. Also, the dragon head has no connection on the Abaj Takalik stela to either a tree or a winged figure. As on Abaj Takalik Stela 5, the figure clasps his left arm to his body, palm directed back to the shoulder. On Abaj Takalik Stelae 1 and 5, the figure wears the knotted-type anklets and stands before a vertical column of hieroglyphs. None of these traits is found at Izapa; indeed they are Maya characteristics. The only agreement in the arrangement of visual traits between Abaj Takalik Stela 1 and the Izapa stelae is the large fractionally represented figure standing on a groundline. The Abaj Takalik stela is definitely not an Izapa-style carving.

Altogether, Abaj Takalik Stela 2 contains only seven traits that appear on the Izapa stelae, including a large, standing figure that is fractionally represented and probably (judging from its occurrence on the other Abaj Takalik stelae) standing on a groundline. The composition is symmetrical and aranged in upper and lower zones. A downward-peering head surrounded by double scrolls fills the upper portion of the stela, and the composition focuses on centrally placed hieroglyphs. On this stela only the large, fractionally represented figure standing on a single groundline agrees with the Izapa traits. Although a symmetrical composition is shown on Abaj Takalik Stela 2, the figures are neither small nor represented in profile. In addition, there is no stela from the site of Izapa with only two large figures arranged on either side of a central element. While part of the Abaj Takalik stela is missing, there is nothing to suggest the occurrence of the two other traits that should occur with the downward-peering head. The overall lack of action on this stela, the emphasis upon the hieroglyphs, the un-Izapa emphasis on small details, and the very limited agreement with the Izapa visual traits groups indicate that Abaj Takalik Stela 2 is not an example of the Izapa art style.

Next, Abaj Takalik Stela 3 (Fig. 43c) (Miles 1965: Fig. 16g)—the upper portion is missing— has only five traits in common with the Izapa stelae. Again, there is a large figure standing on a groundline, wearing a serpent loincloth tie. The dragon head occurs twice at the base of this stela, on both sides of a glyph that is similar, but not the same as, the glyph on Izapa Altar 60 (Norman 1973: Pl. 61). Altar 60 also has a dragon head faintly carved into the section above the glyph. Perhaps there is a connection between the meaning of these two works; unfortunately, the glyph that appears on Izapa Altar 60 does not regularly occur on Izapa stelae and therefore has not been analyzed. As was the case with Abaj Takalik Stelae 1 and 2, the only comparison between Abaj Takalik Stela 3 and the Izapa stelae is the co-occurrence of the large figure standing on a groundline. This evidence is not sufficient to classify the stela as Izapa.

Finally, Abaj Takalik Stela 5 (Fig. 44) shares six traits with the Izapa stelae. Once again two large figures, fractionally represented, stand on a groundline. They are arranged symmetrically, facing centrally placed inscriptions that are an early form of Maya writing (Graham 1977: 196). In addition to the hieroglyphs, Abaj Takalik Stela 5 has three traits that are early Maya and that do not occur on the stelae from Izapa—the tripart kilt, the knotted

anklets, and the hands clasped to the chest, holding a serpent bar. Only the large, fractionally represented figure standing on a groundline agrees with the Izapa use of visual traits. Graham (1977: 196–197) feels that this and other Abaj Takalik stelae "represent a fully developed Maya complex." The presence of Maya traits and the absence of Izapa characteristics support this argument. Graham (1977: 197) reports that the small seated figures on each side of Abaj Takalik Stela 5 bear close resemblance to the seated attendants shown on Izapa Stela 18 "although the figures are rendered in Maya fashion" (1978: 92). Graham (1977: 197) goes on to suggest that the seated figures on Abaj Takalik Stela 5 may indicate a partial chronological overlap between the sculptures of Izapa and Abaj Takalik. Were these Abaj Takalik figures carved at the same time as the rest of the stelae? Certainly the role of seated persons as attendants is an Izapa idea, but Izapa seated figures attend incense burners or other seated figures, not standing figures.

Bilbao Monument 42 (Fig. 40e) might also be considered an early Maya rather than an Izapa carving. The monument features a dragon head upon which a large figure stands. The figure faces to his left unlike those on the Izapa stelae, and because the upper portion is missing, it is impossible to guess if any action occurs. The knotted sandals are Maya (Proskouriakoff 1970: Fig. 30 A1a) as are the tripart kilt or belt ornament and probably the garters (Proskouriakoff 1950: Fig. 29). The placement of the dragon head at the bottom of the scene is the single reference to the Izapa style, and yet the dragon is not even part of a tree or any other reference to the Izapa scheme.

The last work that is considered here is the Chiapa de Corzo Bone 1 (Fig. 40b). This bone carving is included in a study of Izapa-style art by Quirarte (1976: 78) because of the U elements found on the body of the double-headed creature. Quirarte believes that these U elements are references to the jaguar. The Chiapa de Corzo figure does have crocodile hands and a dragon head, but the linking of the dragon head with a masked human presents a creature totally absent on Izapa stelae. Even if the creature could be considered a double-headed serpent, the heads are inappropriate to the Izapa expression of that motif. This bone carving, then, bears some formal but no iconographic references to the Izapa art style.

While all of the works so far discussed bear some visual traits that regularly occur on Izapa stelae, only Kaminaljuyu Stelae 4 and 19 present sufficient evidence for a relationship to Izapa iconography to be included in future analysis of that art style. The Abaj Takalik stelae and Bilbao Monument 42 are probably early Maya, while the emphasis upon the hieroglyphs on El Baul Stela 1 suggests that it, too, is related to the Abaj Takalik stelae. Kaminaljuyu Stelae 10 and 11, El Jobo Stela 1, and the Chiapa de Corzo bone carving are not clearly related to the Izapa style, although the number of similarities between them and the Izapa stelae indicates some borrowing of visual traits.

As a statistical test to determine if Kaminaljuyu Stelae 4 and 19 are members of the Izapa-style works, the NT-SYS computer program was employed once again (Table 7). This time the twelve stelae from sites outside Izapa, and the six visual traits which occur on these works, were coded and added to the data. As before, the enlarged data base was submitted to the "TAXON" operation of the NT-SYS program in order to classify all of the stelae by the occurrence of all visual traits. The dendogram (Table 7) indicates that eight of the works from sites other than Izapa form a group. These works are: Kaminaljuyu Stelae 10 and 11, Bilbao Monument 42, El Baul Stela 1, and Abaj Takalik Stelae 1, 2, 3, and 5. Kaminaljuyu Stelae 4 and 19 are not part of this group; instead they are similar to each other at the 0.4286 level and in turn, these stelae are statistically similar to Izapa Stelae 1, 22, 50, and 67. These related Izapa and Kaminaljuyu stelae emphasize a water-oriented, serpent-holding or wrestling theme (with the exception of Izapa Stela 1, where the serpent appendages are shared with the Kaminaljuyu stelae).

The presence of several Izapa visual traits explains the statistical relationship between the Chiapa de Corzo bone carving and Izapa Stela 25 (0.2667). As previously noted, the low level of similarity, and the context of the traits on the carving from Chiapa de Corzo, do not suggest a strong affiliation for the carving with the Izapa-style works.

Further, El Jobo Stela 1 shares a statistical similarity of 0.5294 with Izapa Stela 21. While it is true that the El Jobo stela has ten visual traits in common with the Izapa works, the theme of beheading is the sole characteristic that is consistent with Izapa iconography. It is this theme that links El Jobo Stela 1 with Izapa Stela 21, yet its representation differs on the two stelae; the El Jobo figure merely holds a decapitated head while the Izapa figure is engaged in overcoming his opponent. Also, the El Jobo stela is not related to the eight grouped stelae from sites near Izapa. That this carving shares the theme of decapitation with Izapa Stela 21 (as well as with Izapa Stelae 3 and 4) is significant but probably exaggerated statistically due to the lack of comparison between the El Jobo stela and the grouped works from Abaj Takalik, Kaminaljuyu, Bilbao, and El Baul.

Interpretation: Reevaluation of Specifically Izapa Visual Traits

When Kaminaljuyu Stelae 4 and 19 are added to the list of Izapa stelae, a final list of specifically Izapa visual traits can be formulated since these two stelae have traits not present on the Izapa stelae. "Specifically Izapa traits" means visual traits that occur only on stelae that are classified as Izapa. They are shown in Table 8.

Limited Distribution of Izapa Visual Traits. Some of these visual traits might be compared to similar traits from other sites, but close inspection reveals the uniqueness of the Izapa representatives. The knife or club, it could be argued, occurs at Bilbao on Monument 21 (Parsons 1969, Vol. 2: Plate 31). This carving has a C_{14} date of A.D. 527 ±

136 (Parsons 1969, Vol. 2: 101), and shows a figure posed unlike any Izapa figures and placed amidst flowering vines. The facial features of this and other Bilbao figures are not of a general type but are specific enough to be portraits, which is uncharacteristic of Izapa work.

Another Izapa visual trait, the falling or diving figure, has comparisons at other sites such as Bilbao and Tulum. However, the figures on Bilbao Monuments 3, 4, 6, and 8 (Parsons 1969, Vol. 2: Plate 32a, c; Plate 33a, c), as well as on other Bilbao monuments, differ significantly from those at Izapa. All of the diving figures at Bilbao have portraitlike realistic faces and gaze outward towards the viewer. Further, the whole figure is presented as if descending, with the body horizontal to the ground. At Tulum the Diving God (Lothrop 1924: Fig. 22) is also unlike the Izapa falling figures. Again, the fairly realistic face of the figure emerges in high relief and gazes towards the viewer. The arms and shoulders of the figure are presented horizontal to the ground while the lower half of the body is oriented at a right angle to the head and shoulders. At Izapa, all diving figures gaze downward or are completely upside down. These figures are fractionally represented and are depicted as a type, not as individuals.

Additional Visual Traits. There are several visual traits that are important at Izapa and that have a limited use at other sites. For instance, crocodile or saurian feet might be included on a list of Izapa visual traits since the only other occurrence of this trait is at Chiapa de Corzo on Bone Carving 1. Scroll-like water at the base of the scene and a variation of the mountain glyph not previously mentioned occurs at Chiapa de Corzo on Stelae 4, 5, and 7 (Quirarte 1973: Fig. 7h, i, and f). Scroll-like water occurs at the base and all over the scene on Tres Zapotes Monument C (Stirling 1943: Pl. 5). Rippling water at the base of the scene is shown on Izapa Stelae 1, 22, 23, and 67 and does not occur elsewhere in this context, although the motif appears at Monte Alban II on

articles such as clay boxes (Bernal 1969: Fig. 32). Yet another visual trait, overlapping of forms, is excluded from a list of specifically Izapa visual traits only because other art styles have used this device; nowhere is overlapping of figures employed to the extent that it occurs in Izapa art.

A visual characteristic that is not easily measured (and therefore has not been coded), but has been mentioned in this paper, is the amount of dramatic action shown on Izapa stelae. Dramatic action does occur elsewhere, such as at Chalcatzingo (Bernal 1969: Fig. 22) and on Maya polychrome vases (M. D. Coe 1973: Cat. nos. 26, 33) where persons are captured and mutilated. At Izapa, however, there are specific Izapa poses for specific actions that are not found at other sites. Also, lively action in general is an important aspect of nearly all of the Izapa carvings.

The list of specifically Izapa visual traits is brief. Of fifty-four visual elements, only fourteen can be identified with the site of Izapa alone: further research and future discoveries may even shorten this list. The premise of this paper, that it is not just the identification of forms but their context that determines the existence of a style, is supported by a brief list of Izapa traits. Izapa art shares motifs with much of Mesoamerica. While there are some striking visual traits unique to the site of Izapa (as the dragon-tree), it is the consistent grouping together of particular forms, or the iconography, that identifies an Izapa art style.

Sculpting Techniques. Finally, the techniques of carving and the artists' approach to rendering forms in stone, are unique for the Izapa stelae. The Izapa technique of stone carving is an important characteristic because of its bearing on the hypothesis that Izapa art was a link between Olmec and Maya styles. Certainly the technical aspects of Izapa carving do not support the notion of an intermediary role. Where monuments from the Olmec heartland are carved with subtly modelled and rounded contours that allow the image to emerge from the stone, the Izapa stones are treated as surfaces upon which images are defined, in most cases, by simply removing the background and adding incised lines for detail. Olmec artists treated a carving as a sculptural entity with some three-dimensional aspects; the Izapa emphasized more two-dimensional qualities of line to the extent that the stelae may be viewed as drawings engraved into stone. In addition, the Olmec artists chose, for both the colossal heads and the stelae, stones that required minimum reshaping. The surfaces of the Olmec stelae, such as Monument 19 (Drucker et al. 1959: Pl. 49; Drucker 1981: 40), were not dressed before carving and the resulting work shows subtle undulations of the original surface.

Izapa and Maya stones were treated as surfaces upon which to apply a design and were therefore prepared before being carved. Still, despite a shared emphasis on two-dimensionality, the Izapa techniques do not compare well to early Maya carving. The Maya figures are carved with crisp, linear, outlined forms rather than with Olmec three-dimensional corporeality, yet they contrast with the Izapa works in the amount of carved rather than incised detail. The Maya works are further distinguished by the use of various levels of carving away of the surface and the fluid quality of body outlines (Proskouriakoff 1950: 102). Also, early Maya works lack the Izapa interest in an extensive use of overlapping, diminution of size, and spatial qualities such as vertical perspective. These artistic conventions are dependent, to some extent, upon the artists' concepts of making images on stone.

Interpretation: Chronology

As shown earlier in this paper there is little good evidence upon which any determination of temporal horizons for the Izapa stelae can be made; in addition, even a comparison of the Izapa visual traits with securely dated works must proceed cautiously, as the result may show the distribution of a trait in time rather than its contemporaneity. It is unfortunate that some of the most comparable works from other sites, like the Izapa

works, do not bear dates. The following discussion of non-Izapa works does not include statistical analysis; rather the works are considered as they relate to a chronological placement of the Izapa art style.

Kaminaljuyu Stelae 4 and 19 are considered as certainly related to the Izapa style, but the dates of these works are not securely determined. Although it bears no date, Miles places Kaminaljuyu Stela 4 in Division 2, corresponding to the Providencia Phase, because the figure represented on this stela wears a chest ornament "which is a close variant of the symbol on a Providencia bowl" as reported to her by E. M. Shook. She also compares the earplug worn by the figure to the Monte Alto jaguar head which has no determined date, rather only a possible assignment to Division 1 (Miles 1965: 250–251). Kaminaljuyu Stela 19 is undated.

In contrast to the Kaminaljuyu stelae, stelae and mural paintings from Oaxaca and stelae from Cerro de las Mesas *do* bear dates or are fairly securely dated. Their similarities with Izapa carvings may only indicate the tenacity or popularity of particular visual traits rather than an actual temporal connection to Izapa.[9] It is, however, tempting to compare some of these works. For instance, a relief carving from Tlacochahuaya in the Valley of Oaxaca, published by Joyce Marcus (1976: Fig. 23) (Fig. 40a) clearly represents a dragon head with a curved snout, stepped mandible, and the single open eye, features that are characteristic of Izapa heads. Marcus assigns the Tlacochahuaya carving to Monte Alban II, although she feels that few parallels can be drawn between stylistic conventions and themes portrayed at Monte Alban and lesser towns in the valley. However, Marcus calls the Tlacochahuaya dragon a "long-nosed god" and notes its stylistic

[9]Norman (1976: 283–321) compares motifs, especially deity masks, from Izapa to corresponding elements on dated and undated works from many Preclassic and Classic sites in Mesoamerica, and suggests possible Izapa influence at Teotihuacan via Monte Alban II (1976: 318–321). Norman's comparisons of individual traits point to a Late Preclassic date for the Izapa monuments.

similarity to the Izapa representations. Another comparison with Monte Alban II is the toponymic glyph (Fig. 33e) with the Izapa jaguar glyphs, although the Monte Alban version incorporates the jaguar glyph as part of a larger design, perhaps involving a house. The hill glyph in the Izapa style is a shape common at Monte Alban II and later, but the use of the glyph appears to be entirely different at the two sites. At Monte Alban the glyph is associated with place indicators; there is no evidence for a similar interpretation at Izapa. There is a downward-peering human-head glyph from Monte Alban I (Caso 1965b: Fig. 4P). Inverted heads also occur at Monte Alban II, and their function appears to be a pictographic representation of fallen lords or gods (Caso 1965b: 937) (Fig. 16b). Thematically, this motif is comparable to the falling or diving figures at Izapa.

The possible connection between Izapa and Monte Alban II is also suggested by two carved slabs from Dainzu, Oaxaca. Although the majority of the carved slabs that decorated the main mound at Dainzu depict tumbling ball players, two show seated figures who wear masks or headdresses and make offerings (Bernal 1968: 248–249). On the first slab (Fig. 46a), a seated human figure wears a cape and what seems to be a dragon headdress from which project heart-shaped leaves. The face of the figure, including a short, somewhat bulbous nose, is similar to those on Izapa Stelae 5 and 21. A hill glyph is present in front of the figure making an offering. Although the nature of the offering is unclear, an Izapa type of scrollwork is attached to, or behind it.

The second Dainzu slab discussed here (Fig. 46b) shows a seated figure wearing the sort of earplugs found at Izapa, (for example on Izapa Stela 5, the figure standing to the right of the tree). The headdress worn by this figure appears to be a stylized jaguar. Easby and Scott (1970: 98) interpret the mask as that of a long-nosed god, however, and there are some parallels with the Izapa dragon head in the stepped mandible and large alveolar curve. The figure wears a loincloth

and holds a small jaguar head on a platter in a gesture of offering. An incense burner may be shown beneath the offering, but that portion of the carving is unclear.

From Monte Alban IIIA, at that time strongly influenced by Teotihuacan, the mural painting on the north wall of Tomb 104 (Caso 1965a: Fig. 30) also shows some affinity to the Izapa style. Although the treatment of the subject is different, the top of the painting portrays felines, below which are entwined serpents. The seated profile figures below wear Izapa rounded bead necklaces and have the right foot tucked under the left thigh as on Izapa Stela 18. Two stelae from Monte Alban IIIB, Stelae 9 and 10, are thematically related to Izapa subject matter by showing a god that descends from the sky and throws something on the earth (Caso 1965a: Fig. 22a–e).

Next, Cerro de las Mesas Stelae 6 and 8 (Stirling 1943: Fig. 11b, c), both dated works, may be compared with the Izapa stelae. Cerro de las Mesas Stela 6 (Fig. 49a) is dated 9.1.12.14.10 (or A.D. 468) and Stela 8 (Fig. 49b) is somewhat later at 9.4.18.16.8. None of the specialists who have examined the Izapa stelae has considered them this late, and as with the Monte Alban IIIA comparisons, the likenesses noted may reflect only the popularity of particular traits.

Cerro de las Mesas Stela 6 deserves some discussion, however. The standing, fractionally represented figure faces right with the right foot forward; he wears winglike appendages, or a costume with an X center, on his back. His elaborate headdress is made up of the long-lipped head as well as an open-mouthed serpent with a bifurcated tongue. Also, the end of the apron or loincloth tie has the same form as the Izapa heart-shaped tree leaves. The formality of the pose and the details of the elaborately costumed figure suggest a formal relationship with Izapa Stela 4. Additional similarities are the presence of diagonal bands on the figure's belt on Cerro de las Mesas Stela 6 and the loincloth tie from Izapa Stela 4, and the two-part scroll motif on the Izapa figure's left wing and on the loincloth of the Cerro de las Mesas figure.

Cerro de las Mesas Stela 8 compares less well to the Izapa examples, but presents a similarly posed figure standing on a jaguar baseline design. The end of the loincloth or apron tie is again the form of Izapa tree leaves, and the ear plug worn by the figure is very much like the Izapa representation of the ornament.

Tres Zapotes Stela D (Fig. 50) and Monument C (Stirling 1943: Plates 17, 18) might also be compared to the Izapa stelae. Although Stela D bears no date, it is tentatively assigned to Olmec III (600–100 B.C.) by Bernal (1969: 112–113). The figures on this monument are much more rubbery than the Izapa figures, but they wear stiff cloaks while they participate in some kind of action that is not portrayed in a highly formalized manner. Above them is a downward-peering head. The whole scene takes place within a rather deeply carved, abstract, jaguar's mouth. On the sides of the jaguar's mouth appear long-lipped heads and thickly curled scrolls that resemble the Izapa examples. A general interest in water-related themes is shared by Monument C at Tres Zapotes and some Izapa stelae. On Monument C a scroll-like water motif is positioned at the base of the scene as in Izapa Stela 5. Surrounded by profuse scroll-work that probably indicates water, weapon-bearing figures tumble and fight. Further, sides C and D feature a rain or water glyph (Fig. 36a) very similar to the glyph shown on the far right of Izapa Stela 12 (Fig. 36b). Much overlapping is used on this carving, and figures are elevated in space rather than standing on a groundline. Also in keeping with the theme of water, a stylized monster-jaguar appears on side A; the protrusion hanging from the monster's mouth may be a huge, bifurcated tongue. In the upper right portion of the same side of this monument is a dragon head with a stepped mandible and scrollwork where a neck and body should be.

It might also be mentioned that Stela C at Tres Zapotes, dated 31 B.C., was removed from its original position; when the stela was set up again, a crude altar was placed in front of it (Bernal 1969: 63). The stela and altar complex is an identifying feature of the Izapan geographic area. If Tres Zapotes, as Bernal suggests (1969: 112), had fallen to the influence of outsiders by the time period he suggests for Stelae C and D, the outside influences might well have been related to Izapa.

A possible indication of chronology that comes from Izapa is information provided by the incense burners found at the site and illustrated on the stelae. Lowe (1965) describes the incense burners illustrated on Izapa Stelae 5, 18, and 24 and compares them to the collection of sherds from Mound 30 and elsewhere at the site. He reports that the cylindrical *incensarios* with projecting points and triangular perforations shown on Stelae 5 and 24 were established as a local type from the Middle Preclassic through the Late Preclassic. While no example of the particular effigy incense burner shown on Stela 18 has been reconstructed from finds at the site, Lowe feels that it is related to other effigy incense burners from the Late Preclassic (Lowe 1965: 54–58).

Comparison of the Izapa stelae with these works from Monte Alban, Cerro de las Mesas, and Tres Zapotes suggests that, at least by Late Preclassic times, Izapa art was probably influencing other sites. While the direction of the influence cannot easily be determined, certainly Izapa was the focus of a highly developed, integrated, and unique art style that could offer much to admire and from which to borrow. Further, the number of similarities to works from Monte Alban II suggests assigning the Izapa stelae to the Late Preclassic.

Conclusions

WHILE THE SOCONUSCO region has not been thoroughly explored, a good deal of attention has been directed toward the sites that have stone monuments. It is therefore noteworthy that there is only one known site with consistently Izapa-style monuments and that during the Late Preclassic, a highly specialized, distinctive art style appeared. The fact that the style includes many widespread Mesoamerican themes in the unique context of depicted coastal estuary-slough-swamp forms suggests a cult focusing on supernatural beings and beliefs related to such an ecosystem. This focus in turn suggests a localized cult developed by a group of people who were highly adapted to the specialized environment, and who had moved to a nearby inland region. The limited geographic spread of this particularly Izapa art further suggests that it may have been quite short-lived.

Of the dozens of sites along the Pacific Coast of Mexico and Guatemala, none compares well to Izapa. Far from being a "connecting link in time and space between the earlier Olmec civilization and the Classic Maya" art styles (M. D. Coe 1962: 100), the Izapa style is unique. Further, the notion that there is a particular link ought to be abandoned, at least until the artistic traditions from many Late Preclassic sites have been defined and examined to determine the extent of regionalization, specialization, and diffusion of the forms and meanings of visual arts during this period. As has been shown by the present study and elsewhere (Panofsky 1960; Kubler 1967, 1969), changes in form and content are not necessarily simultaneous. Without a clear definition of an art style, we can never be sure if we are comparing truly related forms, much less the meanings these forms might have acquired.

Izapa-style art is indeed as distinctive as Matthew Stirling declared in 1943. The stelae present a large inventory of visual traits, some that are shared with much of Mesoamerican art, and others that are unique (such as the tree-dragon, or downward-peering, falling, or diving figures). The organization of these traits for visual expression makes the style unlike any others. Also, the carving techniques and overall emphasis on dramatic actions and water environments are peculiar to this art. Hence, the term Izapa-style ought to be applied only to those works from the site itself and the representatives from other sites that meet the criteria of the definition of the Izapa style. Previous arguments that Izapa was a formal or iconographic link between the Olmec and Maya required the inclusion of works from other Pacific-slopes sites. While there is certainly some evidence for Izapa artistic influence on a few other sites, the Izapa works are more site-specific in form, content, and technique than previously recognized. Present data indicate that it was not a regional style, but a very localized one. Obviously, Izapa art can no longer be considered an intermediary between Olmec and Maya art styles. If it had any influence at all on later Maya art, that influence must be counted as but one among many.

The particular kinds of plants and animals shown on the Izapa stelae help to define the history and chronological placement of Izapa. Coe and Flannery's (1967) study, *Early Cultures and Human Ecology in South Coastal Guatemala*, presents a model (based on floral and faunal remains) that shows a heavy localization and exploitation of the estuary environment. At the site of Salinas La Blanca, collecting was extensive and included mollusks, crabs, and various fruits; fishing in the brackish waters for snook, gar, snapper, catfish, and needle fish supplemented a steady diet of maize grown along the alluvial banks. The Middle Formative saw a climax in population growth supported by these activities. Land clearance moved inland toward the higher rainfall area of the piedmont in the Late Formative (Late Preclassic). In Izapa art the frequent depiction of estuary fauna (such as crocodiles and fish, marsh birds, and jaguars) and flora (for instance the sapodilla, or other fruit-bearing trees) suggests a coastal swamp/lagoon origin for Izapa religious life and its expression in art. Further, the location of Izapa fits the interpretation that Coe and Flannery present for a population shift inland in the Late Preclassic. Perhaps Izapa priest-administrators had a new ceremonial center built over a minor Middle Preclassic site.

Izapa art was probably short-lived as well as highly specialized. The localization of the Izapa style suggests a fairly short period for the manufacture of the stone monuments. The distribution of Izapa-style carvings is limited to Izapa. The only two stelae from Kaminaljuyu—Stelae 4 and 19—that may be considered Izapa might have been manufactured by an Izapa artist recruited or dragooned to the highlands.

As previously demonstrated, comparisons that can be made between the works from Izapa, Monte Alban II, and Tres Zapotes support a Late Preclassic date for the carvings. In addition, comparison with some very early Maya works, Stelae 1, 2, 3, and 5 from Abaj Takalik, shows that the Izapa stelae lack Maya inscriptions and the costume details that characterized the regional Protoclassic. An acceptance of a rather late Late Preclassic date helps to explain the coherence and the limited geographic spread of the Izapa style (cf. Fig. 2). Probably all or most of the stelae were erected over a short period of time and contemporary with the tremendous building activity that so greatly enlarged the site in Late Preclassic times (Ekholm 1969: 4) and that reflected an overall growth in Izapa culture. Although the art style we call Izapa was probably begun and reached its highest development during Mesoamerica's Late Preclassic period of regionalization (Pires-Ferreira 1976a: 304), it was a strongly formulated, cohesive, and unique local phenomenon.

Tables

TABLE 1. DISTRIBUTION OF VISUAL TRAITS BY STELAE AND BY GROUPS OF STELAE

TRAIT GROUPS	STELAE GROUPS → Traits	1	2			3			4			5 (Stelae)							6			7			
		1	23	6	26	8	10	27	14	18	24	2	4	11	3	60	7	21	5	12	25	9	22	67	50
1	FSTAN	•			•		•	•			•	•	•	•	•	•	•	•	•		•	•	•	•	•
	FLARG	•	•	•	•	•	•	•	•	•	•	•	•	•	•	•	•	•	•	•	•	•	•	•	•
	SPLAN	•		•		•	•	•		•	•	•		•	•	•		•	•	•	•		•	•	•
	SOVER					•	•			•		•		•	•			•	•	•	•		•	•	•
	FSTIN			•		•	•	•			•			•		•	•	•					•	•	•
	FFR₁P					•	•					•	•	•	•	•		•				•	•	•	•
	SVERT		•								•	•						•	•		•	•	•	•	•
2	FPROF	•	•	•	•	•	•	•	•	•	•	•				•	•		•	•	•	•	•	•2	•
	FSMAL					•	•		•	•	•	•						•	•	•		•	•	•	
	SSYMT		•		•				•	•		•	•	•					•	•	•	•	•		
3	DWRST																						•	•	•
	ASERP														•						•		•	•2	•
	AFISH	•																	•				•	•	
	TWBLW	•	•																				•	•	
	HOPOS	•	•																				•	•	
	HSEYE	•	•												•			•	•				•		•
4	FPRST								•	•	•								•	•					
	TINBR								•	•									•	•					
	CNEKL								•	•								•	•						
5	FFODV		•					•				•	•												
	CTBLT		•									•	•	•											
	SABBL											•	•							•					
	AWING							•				•	•	•		•					•				
	ACRFT			•								•	•2	•		•					•				
6	DBEHD												•	•		•		•							
	TKNIF												•	•		•		•							
	HDNPR												•				•								
7	DCHLD																		•			•			
	CCLOK																		•			•			•
	TBATN						•															•			
8	DMOTH			•											•	•									
	ABFTM		•	•	•					•					•		•								
	GBOAT		•	•	•																				
9	AESER													•				•	•	•					
	GMTNS			•															•	•					
	GJAGU																		•	•					
	CANKW	•		•						•		•	•	•							•			•	
	TWFAL	•	•	•															•	•					
	AFINS	•																	•						
10	ABIRD																		•		•				
	TTRLA						•												•	•	•				
	TTRDR						•	•				•							•	•					
11	TTRLB						•					•													
	TFRUT						•					•							•						
	HDRAG						•	•				•							•						
	AJAGU							•	•						•			•		•			•		
	GHILL								•														•	•	
	ASAPD	•		•																					•
	CBPPD	•											•	•	•										
	TWABV			•															•						
	TBLUD																		•	•	•				
	GKANC						•	•																	
	SRECS						•	•	•																
	ASSER		•		•					•							•								

52

TABLE 2. CLUSTERS OF VARIABLES, OR VISUAL TRAITS, BY STELAE AND GROUPS OF STELAE

```
      -0.015    0.135    0.285    0.435    0.585    0.735    0.885    1.035
       I--------I--------I--------I--------I--------I--------I--------I
```

IDENT	LEVEL	TRAIT GROUPS
FSTAN001	0.7500	1
FLARG007	0.8261	
SPLAN049	0.6471	
SOVER054	0.5789	
FSTIN003	0.4286	
FFRRP006	0.5000	
SVERT048	0.2941	
FPROF005	0.5556	2
FSMAL008	0.4500	
SSYMT046	0.1111	
DWRST009	0.6000	3
ASERP018	0.2500	
AFISH019	0.8000	
TWBLW030	0.6000	
HOPOS039	0.3750	
HSEYE037	0.1053	
AJAGU017	0.4000	
GHILL045	0.0	
FPRST002	0.8000	4
TINBR029	0.6000	
CNEKL024	0.1667	
ASSER021	0.0	
FFODV004	0.6000	5
CTBLT026	0.6000	
SABBL050	0.2857	
AWING013	0.7143	
ACRFT014	0.1250	
DBEHD010	1.0000	6
TKNIF027	0.3333	
HDNPR040	0.0	
DCHLD011	0.3333	7
CCLOK023	0.3333	
TBATN028	0.0	
DMOTH012	0.3333	8
ABFTM015	0.7500	
GBOAT041	0.1667	
ASAPD016	0.2500	
CBPPD051	0.0	
AESER020	0.5000	9
GMTNS042	1.0000	
GJAGU043	0.2000	
CANKW025	0.4444	
TWFAL032	0.2222	
AFINS053	0.1111	
ABIRD022	1.0000	10
TTRLA034	0.5000	
TTRDR033	0.0	
TWABV031	0.2500	
TBLUD052	0.0	
TTRLB035	0.6667	11
TFRUT036	0.4000	
HDRAG038	0.1667	
GKANC044	0.6667	
SRECS047		

```
       I--------I--------I--------I--------I--------I--------I--------I   IDENT    LEVEL
      -0.015    0.135    0.285    0.435    0.585    0.735    0.885    1.035
```

53

TABLE 3. GROUPS OF IZAPA STELAE

```
0    -0.060      0.090       0.240       0.390       0.540       0.690       0.840     0.990                                      STELA
     I--------I---------I---------I---------I---------I---------I---------I    IDENT        LEVEL    GROUP
                                  .------------------------------------------  STELA001     0.3158  ┐
                        I                                                                           │ 1
                        .------L------------------------------------------     STELA023     0.2000  ┘
              I
              I                       .-----------------------------------     STELA006     0.4286  ┐
              I               I                                                                     │ 2
              .------L------------------L---------------------------------     STELA026     0.0909  ┘
         I
         I                       .---------------------------------------      STELA008     0.4615  ┐
         I                   I                                                                      │
         I             .------L-----------------------------------------      STELA010     0.3889  │ 3
         I            I                                                                             │
         I      .------------L---------------------------------------          STELA027     0.1765  ┘
         I      I
         I      I             .-----------------------------------------       STELA014     0.3636  ┐
         I      I       I                                                                           │
         I      I       I                   .-----------------------------     STELA018     0.6667  │ 4
         I      I       I             I                                                             │
         .--L------L---------L---------------------L-------------------------  STELA024     0.0476  ┘
    I
    I                             .-----------------------------------         STELA002     0.5455  ┐
    I                     I                                                                         │
    I                     .-----------L-----------------------------------     STELA004     0.3636  │
    I                 I                                                                             │
    I           .------L-------------------------------------------           STELA011     0.2222  │
    I           I                                                                                  │
    I           I             .---------------------------------               STELA003     0.3810  │ 5
    I           I       I                                                                           │
    I           I       I             .-----------------------               STELA007     0.6364  │
    I           I       I       I                                                                   │
    I           I       I       .-----------L-------------------------         STELA060     0.4286  │
    I           I       I   I                                                                       │
    I     .------L---------L---L---------------------------------------        STELA021     0.1071  ┘
    I     I
    I     I                       .------------------------------------        STELA005     0.4643  ┐
    I     I                 I                                                                        │
    I     I           .------------L----------------------------------        STELA012     0.2609  │ 6
    I     I       I                                                                                  │
    I     I       .------L----------------------------------------           STELA025     0.1538  ┘
    I     I  I
    I     I  I             .-------------------------------------             STELA009     0.3333  ┐
    I     I  I       I                                                                               │
    I     I  I       I                       .-------                        STELA022     0.8824  │ 7
    I     I  I       I                   I                                                           │
    I     I  I       I             .---------------------------L------        STELA067     0.4737  ┘
    I     I  I       I       I                                                                       
-------L---L--L---------L-------L-------------------------------------         STELA050
```

```
     I--------I---------I---------I---------I---------I---------I---------I    IDENT        LEVEL
     -0.060      0.090       0.240       0.390       0.540       0.690       0.840     0.990
```

54

TABLE 4. VISUAL TRAITS THAT OCCUR REGULARLY ON IZAPA STELAE
AND THAT APPEAR ON STELAE FROM RELATED SITES

Abbreviations for the sites are: AT, Abaj Takalik: K, Kaminaljuyu; B, Bilbao; ElB, El Baul; J, El Jobo; TZ, Tres Zapotes; CC, Chiapa de Corzo (bone carving); T, Tikal.

Code	Description	Stelae upon which traits occur and location of figures in the text
FSTAN	standing figure	AT 1 (Fig. 43a), AT 2 (Fig. 45a), AT 3 (Fig. 43c), AT 5 (Fig. 44); K 4 (Fig. 40c), K 10 (Fig. 42), K 11 (Fig. 41b); B 42 (Fig. 40e); ElB 1 (Fig. 43b); J 1 (Fig. 41a).
FLARG	large figure	AT 1 (Fig. 43a), AT 2 (Fig. 45a), AT 3 (Fig. 43c), AT 5 (Fig. 44); K 4 (Fig. 40c), K 10 (Fig. 42), K 11 (Fig. 41b), K 19 (Fig. 40d); B 42 (Fig. 40e): ElB 1 (Fig. 43b); J 1 (Fig. 41a).
FFRRP	fractional representation of figure	AT 1 (Fig. 43a), AT 2 (Fig. 45a), AT 5 (Fig. 44); K 10 (Fig. 42), K 11 (Fig. 41b), K 19 (Fig. 40d); J 1 (Fig. 41a); ElB 1 (Fig. 43b).
FPROF	figure shown in profile or three-quarter view	K 10 (Fig. 42); CC 1 (Fig. 40b); J 1 (Fig. 41a).
FSTIN	seated individual figure	K 19 (Fig. 40d); J 1 (Fig. 41a).
FSMAL	small figures	J 1 (Fig. 41a).
CBPPD	knee-pads	K 4 (Fig. 40c), K 19 (Fig. 40d); J 1 (Fig. 41a).
TBATN	curved staff or stave	K 11 (Fig. 41b); ElB 1 (Fig. 43b); J 1 (Fig. 41a).
HDNPR	downward-peering head	AT 2 (Fig. 45a); K 11 (Fig. 41b); ElB 1 (Fig. 43b); TZ D (Fig. 50); T 29 (Fig. 45b).
DBEHD	figure posed as if to behead someone	K 10 (Fig. 42); J 1 (Fig. 41a).
AJAGU	jaguar	AT 1 (Fig. 43a).
ASERP	single-headed serpent	AT 5 (Fig. 44, serpent bar); K 19 (Fig. 40d).
SPLAN	shallow spatial depth	AT 1 (Fig. 43a), AT 2 (Fig. 45a), AT 3 (Fig. 43c), AT 5 (Fig. 44); K 11 (Fig. 41b); B 42 (Fig. 40e); ElB 1 (Fig. 43b); J 1 (Fig. 41a).
SSYMT	symmetrical composition	AT 2 (Fig. 45a), AT 5 (Fig. 44); K 11 (Fig. 41b), K 19 (Fig. 40d).
CCLOK	stiff cloak	K 11 (Fig. 41b); TZ D (Fig. 50).

TABLE 5. TYPICALLY IZAPA VISUAL TRAITS THAT OCCUR ON STELAE FROM RELATED SITES

Abbreviations for the sites are: AT, Abaj Takalik; K, Kaminaljuyu; B, Bilbao; J, El Jobo; CC, Chiapa de Corzo (bone carving).

Code	Description	Stelae upon which traits occur and location of figures in the text
SABBL	picture plane is divided into upper and lower regions, figures stand on or emerge from top- and baseline designs.	AT 2 (Fig. 45a); ElB 1 (Fig. 43b).
CANKW	band-type anklets or bracelets	ElB 1 (Fig. 43b); CC 1 (Fig. 40b).
HDRAG	dragon head	AT 1 (Fig. 43a), AT 3 (Fig. 43c); K 10 (Fig. 42), K 11 (Fig. 41b); B 42 (Fig. 40e); CC 1 (Fig. 40b).
AFINS	attached fins	K 4 (Fig. 40c), K 19 (Fig. 40d).
ACRFT	crocodile feet	K 4 (Fig. 40c), K 19 (Fig. 40d); CC 1 (Fig. 40b).
SOVER	overlapping of forms	K 4 (Fig. 40c), K 19 (Fig. 40d).
TWFAL	falling water	K 4 (Fig. 40c), K 19 (Fig. 40d); ElB 1 (Fig. 43b).
HSEYE	scroll-eyed head	K 4 (Fig. 40c), K 19 (Fig. 40d); ElB 1 (Fig. 43b); J 1 (Fig. 41a); CC 1 (Fig. 40b).
SVERT	vertical perspective	K 4 (Fig. 40c), K 19 (Fig. 40d).
DWRST	the act of holding or wrestling a serpent	K 4? (Fig. 40c), K 19 (Fig. 40d).
AWING	wings or winglike appendages worn by the figure	K 10 (Fig. 42).
CTBLT	bifurcated-tongue loincloth tie or belt	K 11 (Fig. 41b).
TTRLA	heart-shaped tree leaves	K 11 (Fig. 41b).
ASAPD	serpent appendages	AT 1 (Fig. 43a), AT 3 (Fig. 43c); K 4 (Fig. 40c), K 19 (Fig. 40d).

56

TABLE 6. VISUAL TRAITS FOUND ONLY ON STELAE FROM SITES RELATED TO IZAPA

Abbreviations for the sites are: AT, Abaj Takalik; K, Kaminaljuyu; B, Bilbao; ElB, El Baul; J, El Jobo; T, Tikal.

Code	Description	Stelae upon which traits occur and location of figures in the text
CKILT	kilt or tripart belt	AT 5 (Fig. 44); B 42 (Fig. 40e).
CKNTA	knotted anklets	AT 1 (Fig. 43a), AT 5 (Fig. 44); K 11 (Fig. 41b); J 1 (Fig. 41a).
DHDCS	figure holding one or both arms to chest, with fingers directed outward	AT 1 (Fig. 43a), AT 5 (Fig. 44); K 11 (Fig. 41b); J 1 (Fig. 41a).
THEIR	vertically arranged hieroglyphs	AT 1 (Fig. 43a), AT 2 (Fig. 45a), AT 5 (Fig. 44); ElB 1 (Fig. 43b); K 10 (Fig. 42).
SMULT	multiple levels of carving	K 10 (Fig. 42), K 11 (Fig. 41b).
TFLIN	tripart club or hatchet	K 10 (Fig. 42), K 11 (Fig. 41b).

TABLE 7. IZAPA STELAE AND STELAE FROM RELATED SITES CLUSTERED BY ALL VARIABLES

Abbreviations for the sites are: K, Kaminaljuyu; AT, Abaj Takalik; CC, Chiapa de Corzo; ElB, El Baul; B, Bilbao; J, El Jobo; all others are Izapa.

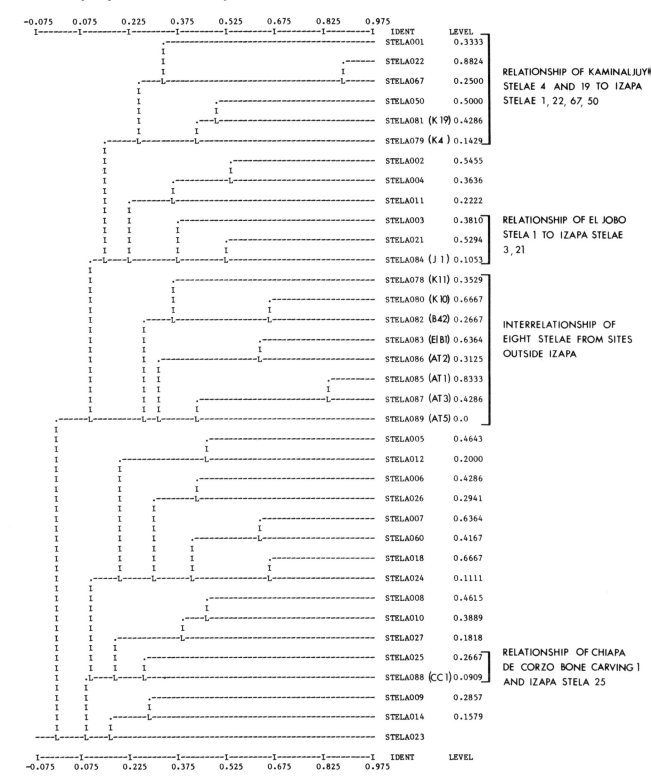

TABLE 8. SPECIFICALLY IZAPA VISUAL TRAITS

Stelae from Kaminaljuyu are preceded by a K; all other stelae are Izapa.

Code	Description	Izapa stelae and figures in the text
FFODV	falling or diving figure	2 (Fig. 14a), 4 (Fig. 15b), 23 (Fig. 15a), 27 (Fig. 14b).
DWRST	the act of holding or wrestling a serpent	22 (Figs. 8a, 9b), 50 (Fig. 5b), 67 (Figs. 8b, 9a), K 4 (Fig. 40c), K 19 (Fig. 40d).
DMOTH	holding something in the mouth or on the tongue	3 (Fig. 21a), 6 (Fig. 21c), 11 (Fig. 21b).
AESER	double-headed earth serpent	5 (Fig. 23a), 7 (Fig. 24b), 11 (Fig. 22a), 12 (Fig. 22b).
ASSER	double-headed sky serpent	7 (Fig. 24a), 18 (Fig. 25b), 23 (Fig. 25a), 26 (Fig. 23b).
AWING	wings or winglike appendages worn by the figure	2 (Fig. 14a), 4 (Fig. 15b), 11 (Fig. 16a), 25 (Fig. 13b), 27 (Fig. 14b), 60 (Fig. 14c).
HOPOS	opposing bodiless heads at the base of the scene	1 (Fig. 30b), 22 (Fig. 31c), 23 (Fig. 30a), 67 (Fig. 31b).
TWABV	water above, at the top of the scene	21 (Fig. 35a), 26 (Fig. 35b).
TKNIF	knife or club	3 (Fig. 3b), 4 (Fig. 3a), 21 (Fig. 4a).
TTRDR	tree-dragon	2 (Fig. 39a), 5 (Fig. 38b), 10 (Fig. 38c), 25 (Fig. 39b), 27 (Fig. 39c).
TFRUT	fruit	2 (Fig. 39a), 5 (Fig. 38b), 27 (Fig. 27c).
GBOAT	canoe-shaped U element with human head	6 (Fig. 32f), 3 (Fig. 32e), 26 (Fig. 32g).

Figures

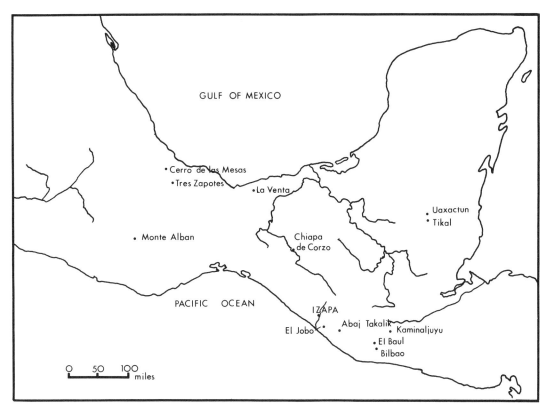

Fig. 1   Map of Mexico and Guatemala with cited archaeological sites.

	Present Study	Miles 1965	Norman 1973	M.D. Coe 1962	Bernal 1969	Parsons 1969	Ekholm 1969	Quirarte 1973
Middle Classic — AD 600								
.... 400								
Early Classic — 200								
.... —		Division 4 Arenal Ceramics	Proto-Classic					
Proto-Classic 1	Late Pre-Classic	Division 3 Miraflores Ceramics	Late Pre-Classic	Late Formative		Proto-Classic	Late Pre-Classic ?	Proto-Classic
Late Pre-Classic — 200		Division 2 Providencia Ceramics			Late Pre-Classic			Late Pre-Classic
.... 400		Division 1 Las Charcas, Arevalo Ceramics			Olmec III		Middle Pre-Classic Duende Phase	
Middle Pre-Classic 600								
.... 800								
Early Pre-Classic BC								

Fig. 2   Time allocation of Izapa art: comparison with other studies.

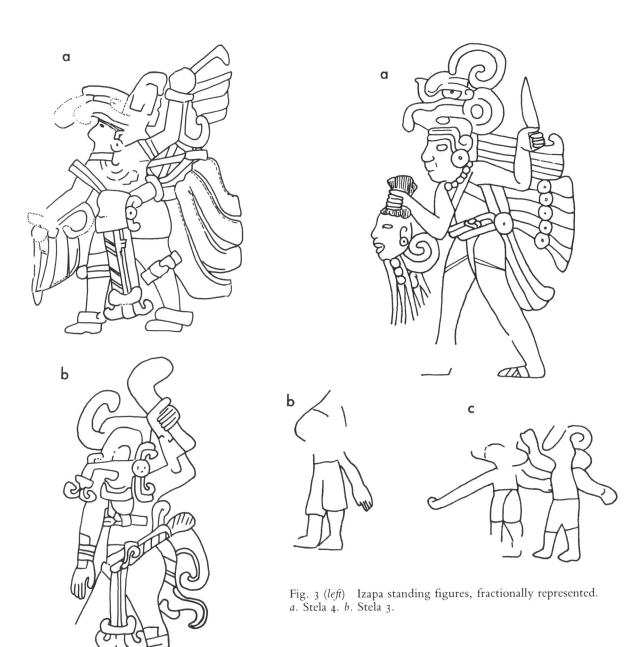

Fig. 3 (*left*) Izapa standing figures, fractionally represented.
a. Stela 4. *b*. Stela 3.

Fig. 4 (*above*) Izapa standing figures, fractionally represented.
a. Stela 21. *b*. Stela 27. *c*. Stela 10.

Fig. 5 (*above*) Izapa standing figures. *a*. Stela 9. *b*. Stela 50.

Fig. 6 (*right*) Izapa standing figures. *a*. Stela 1. *b, c*. Stela 5. *d*. Stela 2.

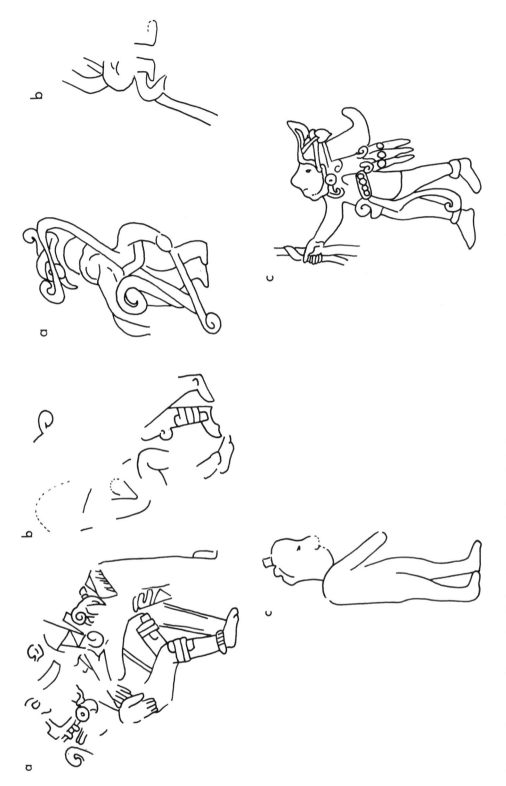

Fig. 7 Izapa standing and reclining figures. *a.* Stela 60. *b.* Stela 7. *c.* Stela 27.

Fig. 8 Izapa standing figures. *a.* Stela 22. *b.* Stela 67. *c.* Stela 25.

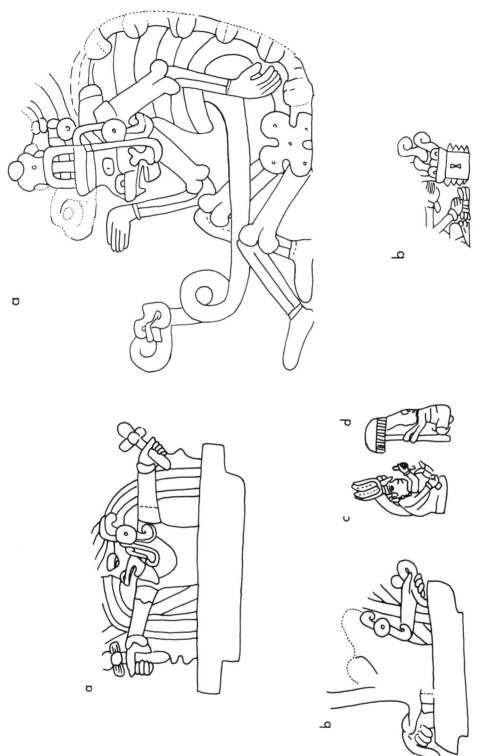

a

b

Fig. 9 Izapa seated figures. *a.* Stela 67. *b.* Stela. 22. *c, d.* Stela 5.

a

b

c d

Fig. 10 Izapa seated figures. *a.* Stela 50. *b.* Stela 24.

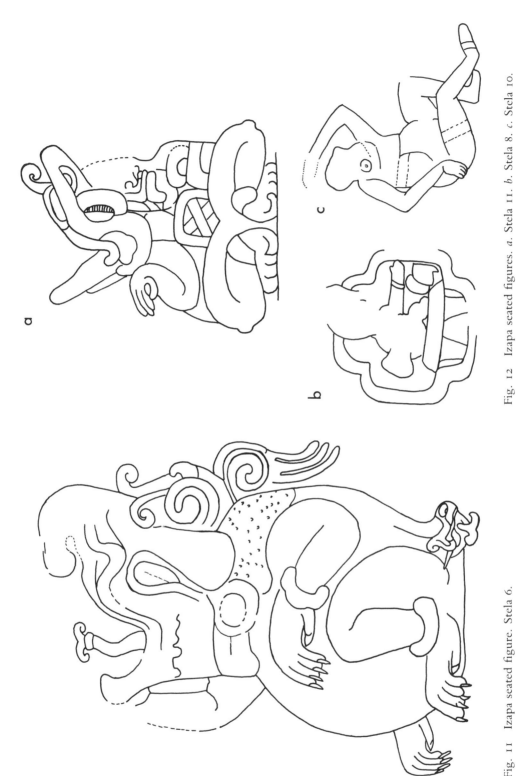

Fig. 12 Izapa seated figures. *a.* Stela 11. *b.* Stela 8. *c.* Stela 10.

Fig. 11 Izapa seated figure. Stela 6.

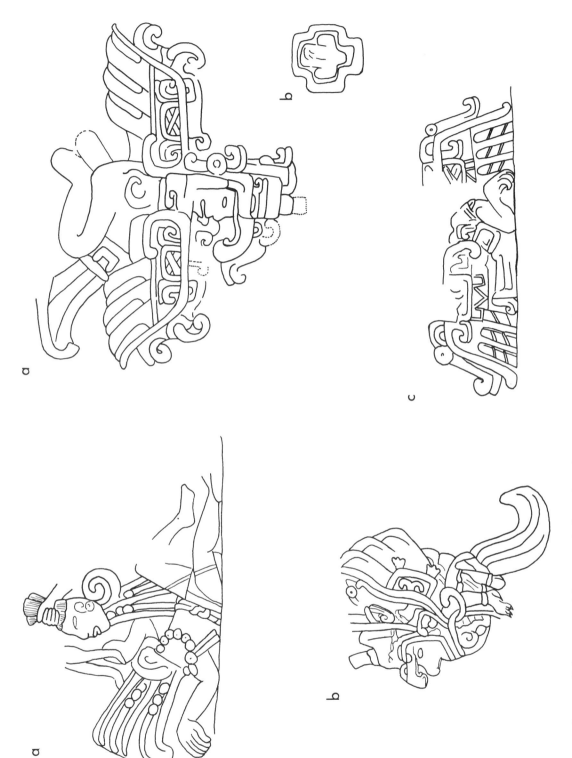

Fig. 13 Izapa reclining or seated figures. *a.* Stela 21. *b.* Stela 25.

Fig. 14 Izapa diving or fallen figures. *a.* Stela 2. *b.* Stela 27. *c.* Stela 60.

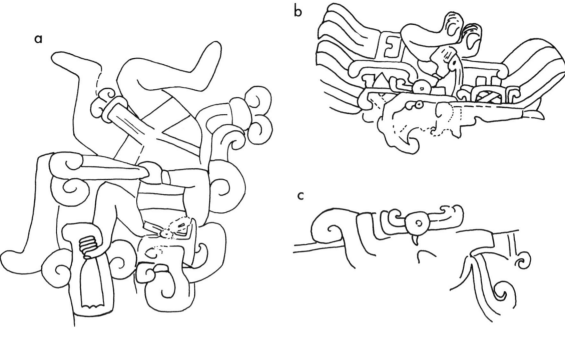

Fig. 15 (*above*) Izapa diving figures and downward-peering heads. *a*. Stela 23. *b*. Stela 4. *c*. Stela 7.

Fig. 16 (*right*) Izapa standing figure and Fallen Lord, Monte Alban. *a*. Stela 11. *b*. Fallen Lord from Mound J, Monte Alban (after Bernal 1969: Fig. 29a).

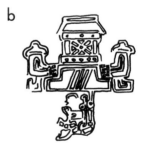

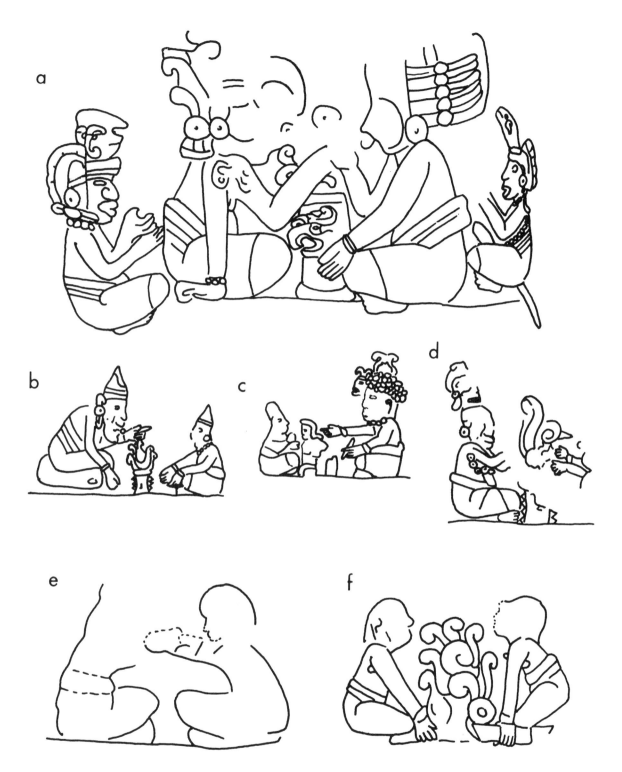

Fig. 17 Izapa figures, seated pairs. *a*. Stela 18. *b, c.* Stela 5. *d.* Stela 24. *e.* Stela 14. *f.* Stela 12.

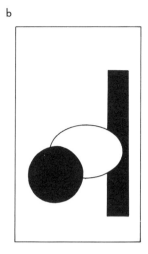

Fig. 18 Izapa organization of ground or picture plane. *a*. Shallow spatial depth. *b*. Overlapping of figures.

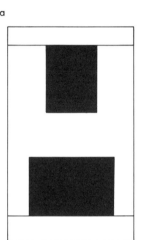

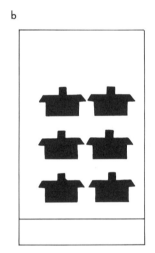

Fig. 19 Izapa organization of ground or picture plane. *a*. Picture plane is divided into two regions vertically, as figures rest on or emerge from top- and baseline designs. *b*. Vertical perspective, where further images are higher in the picture plane and figures do not rest on a groundline.

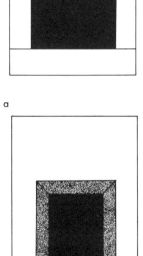

Fig. 20 Izapa organization of ground or picture plane. *a*. Recessional depth, a carved extension of the actual space in which the viewer stands. *b*. Symmetrical arrangement of forms in space.

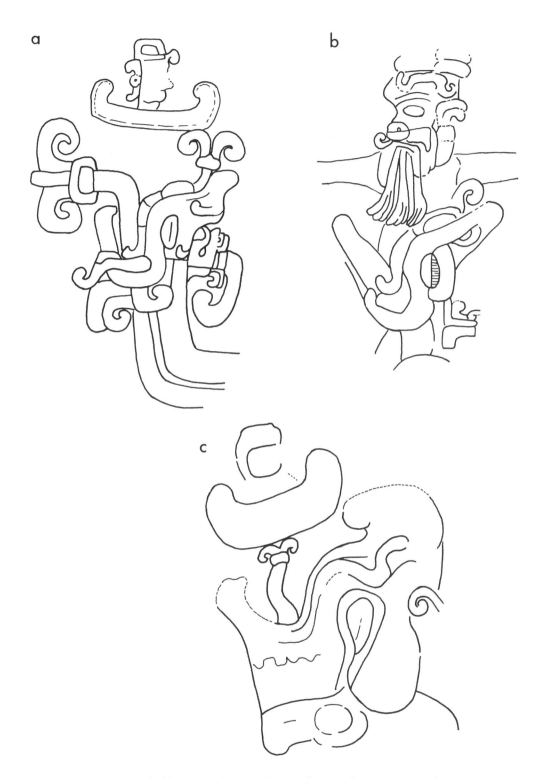

Fig. 21   Izapa action, holding something in the mouth or on the tongue. *a*. Stela 3. *b*. Stela 11.
c. Stela 6.

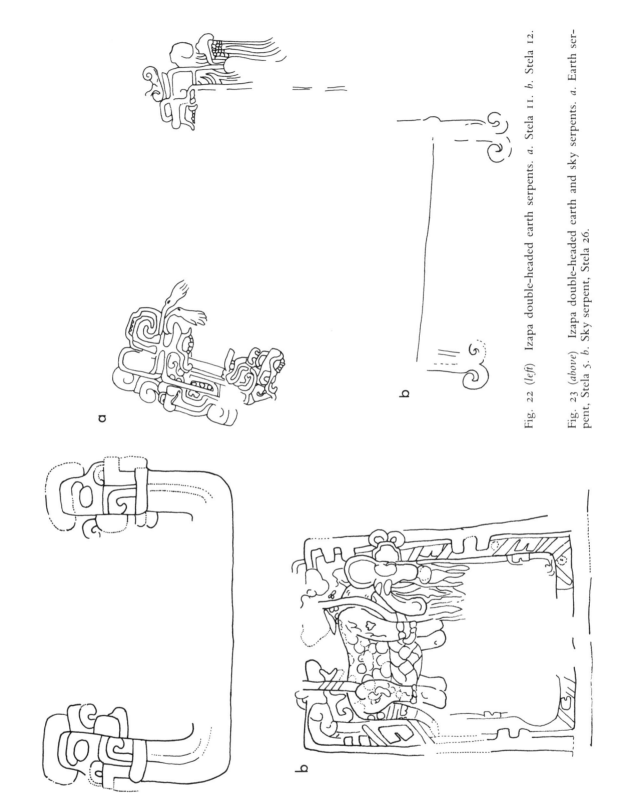

Fig. 22 (*left*) Izapa double-headed earth serpents. *a.* Stela 11. *b.* Stela 12.

Fig. 23 (*above*) Izapa double-headed earth and sky serpents. *a.* Earth serpent, Stela 5. *b.* Sky serpent, Stela 26.

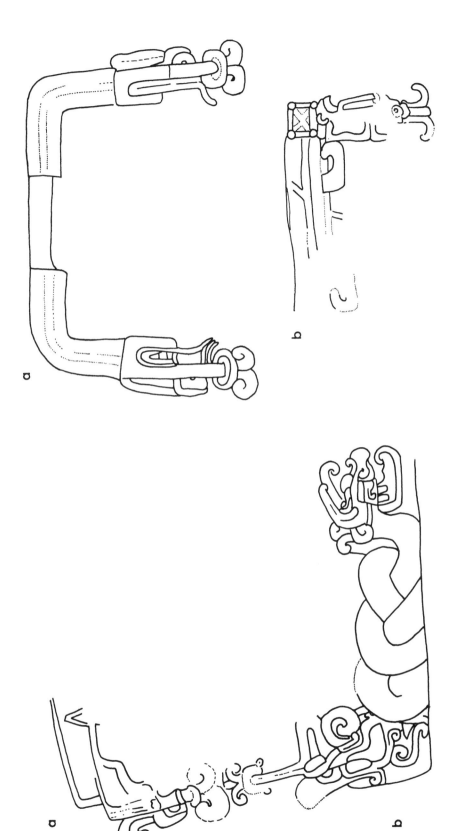

Fig. 24 Izapa double-headed earth and sky serpents. *a*. Sky serpent, Stela 7. *b*. Earth serpent, Stela 7.

Fig. 25 Izapa double-headed sky serpents. *a*. Stela 23. *b*. Stela 18.

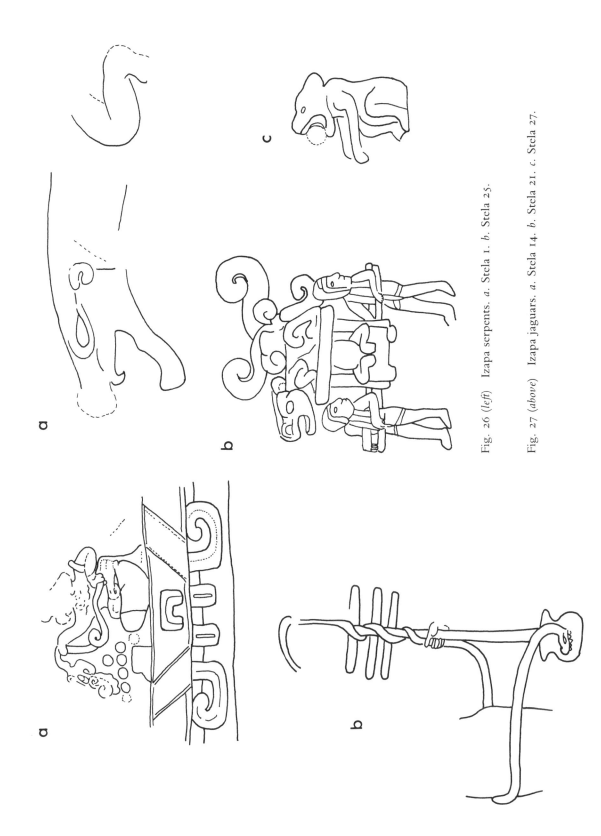

Fig. 26 (*left*) Izapa serpents. *a.* Stela 1. *b.* Stela 25.

Fig. 27 (*above*) Izapa jaguars. *a.* Stela 14. *b.* Stela 21. *c.* Stela 27.

Fig. 28   Izapa fish and birds. *a.* Stela 67. *b.* Stela 5.
c, d. Stela 1. *e.* Stela 22. *f, g.* Stela 5. *h.* Stela 25.

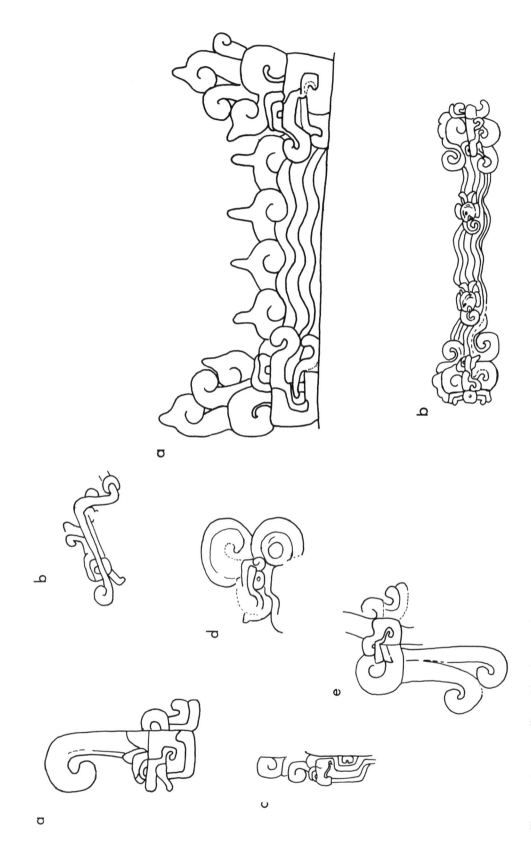

Fig. 29 Izapa scroll-eyed heads. *a.* Stela 3. *b.* Stela 22. *c.* Stela 5. *d.* Stela 21. *e.* Stela 50.

Fig. 30 Izapa opposing and scroll-eyed heads with water motifs that occur at the base of the scene. *a.* Stela 23. *b.* Stela 1.

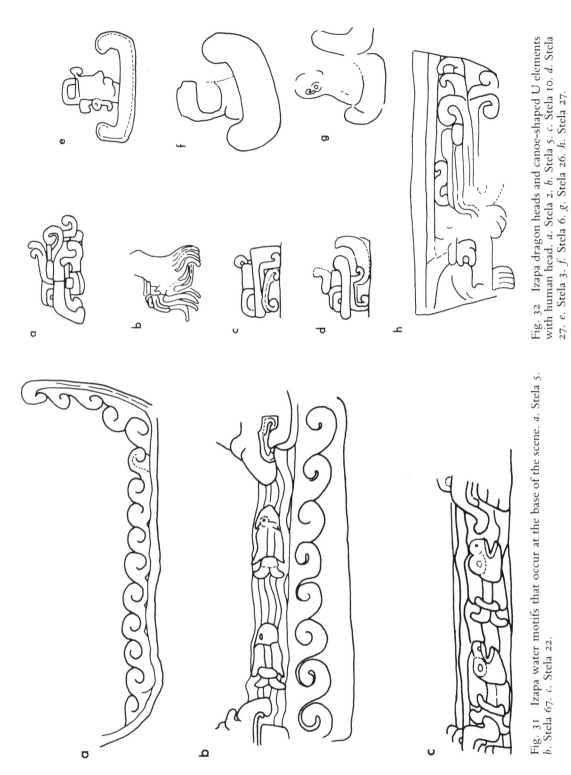

Fig. 32 Izapa dragon heads and canoe-shaped U elements with human head. *a.* Stela 2. *b.* Stela 5. *c.* Stela 10. *d.* Stela 27. *e.* Stela 3. *f.* Stela 6. *g.* Stela 26. *h.* Stela 27.

Fig. 31 Izapa water motifs that occur at the base of the scene. *a.* Stela 5. *b.* Stela 67. *c.* Stela 22.

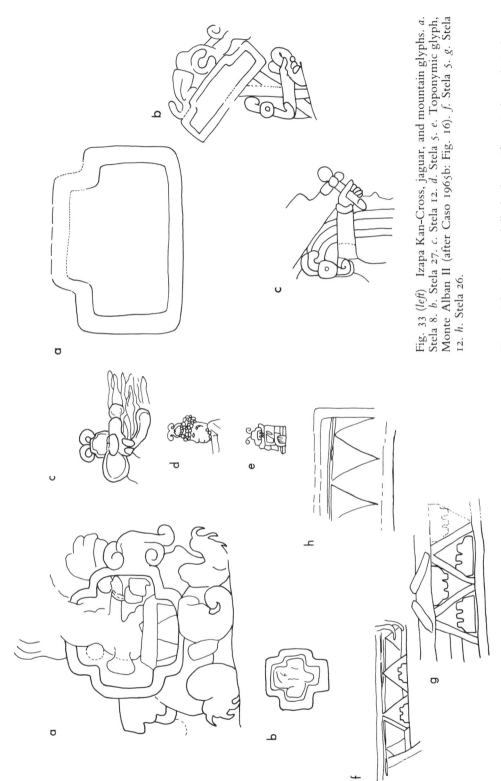

Fig. 33 (*left*) Izapa Kan-Cross, jaguar, and mountain glyphs. *a.* Stela 8. *b.* Stela 27. *c.* Stela 12. *d.* Stela 5. *e.* Toponymic glyph, Monte Alban II (after Caso 1965b: Fig. 16). *f.* Stela 5. *g.* Stela 12. *h.* Stela 26.

Fig. 34 (*above*) Izapa hill glyph motifs. *a.* Stela 14. *b.* Stela 22. *c.* Stela 67.

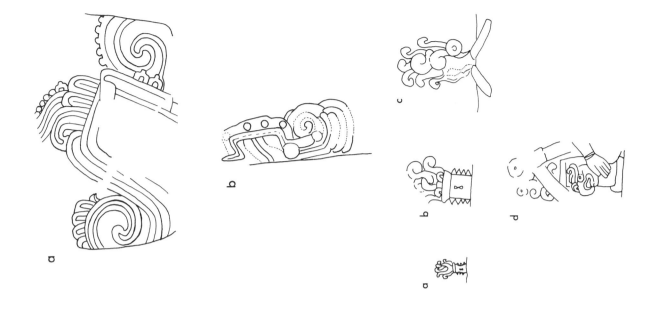

Fig. 35 (*above*) Izapa water motifs. *a.* Stela 21. *b.* Stela 26. *c.* Stela 1. *d.* Stela 5. *e.* Stela 6.

Fig. 36 (*above right*) Rain or water motifs. *a.* Monument C, Tres Zapotes (after Stirling 1943: Plates 18a, b). *b.* Stela 12, Izapa.

Fig. 37 (*right*) Izapa incense burners and fire. *a.* Stela 5. *b.* Stela 24. *c.* Stela 12. *d.* Stela 18.

c

a

b

c

a

b

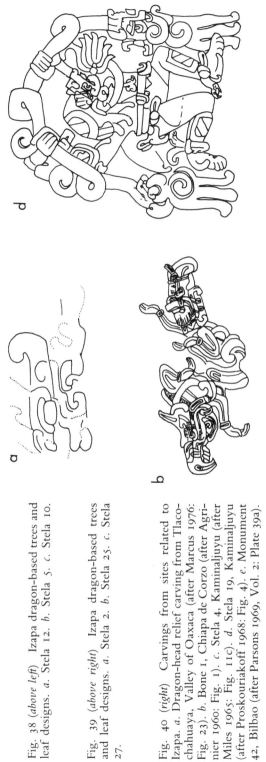

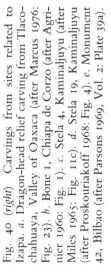

Fig. 38 (*above left*) Izapa dragon-based trees and leaf designs. *a.* Stela 12. *b.* Stela 5. *c.* Stela 10.

Fig. 39 (*above right*) Izapa dragon-based trees and leaf designs. *a.* Stela 2. *b.* Stela 25. *c.* Stela 27.

Fig. 40 (*right*) Carvings from sites related to Izapa. *a.* Dragon-head relief carving from Tlaco-chahuaya, Valley of Oaxaca (after Marcus 1976: Fig. 23). *b.* Bone 1, Chiapa de Corzo (after Agri-nier 1960: Fig. 1). *c.* Stela 4, Kaminaljuyu (after Miles 1965: Fig. 11c). *d.* Stela 19, Kaminaljuyu (after Proskouriakoff 1968: Fig. 4). *e.* Monument 42, Bilbao (after Parsons 1969, Vol. 2: Plate 39a).

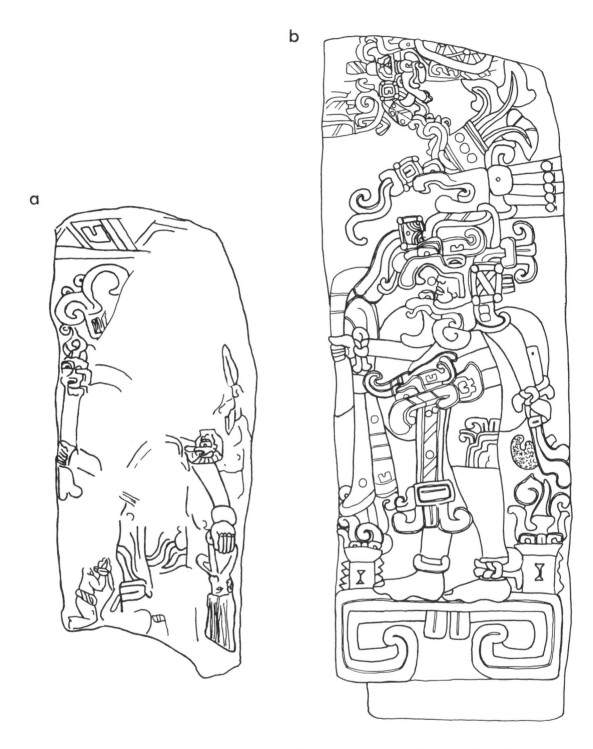

Fig. 41   Carvings from sites related to Izapa. *a*. Stela 1, El Jobo (after Miles 1965: Fig. 15b). *b*. Stela 11, Kaminaljuyu (after Miles 1965: Fig. 15a).

Fig. 42   Stela 10, Kaminaljuyu (from M. D. Coe 1976: Fig. 10).

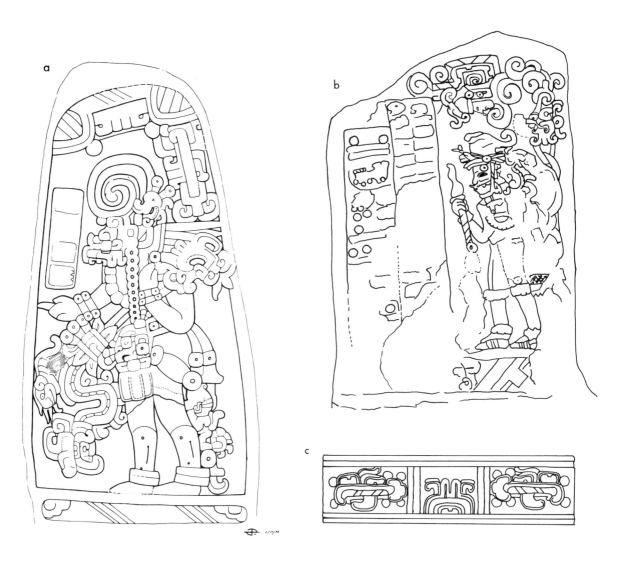

Fig. 43 Carvings from Abaj Takalik and El Baul. *a.* Stela 1, Abaj Takalik. (The knotted anklets do not show here.) Drawing by James Porter, courtesy of John Graham, Archaeological Research Facility, Department of Anthropology, University of California, Berkeley. *b.* Stela 1, El Baul (after Paddock 1966: Fig. 63). *c.* Stela 3, Abaj Takalik (after Miles 1965: Fig. 8g).

Fig. 44   Abaj Takalik, Stela 5. Photograph courtesy of John Graham.

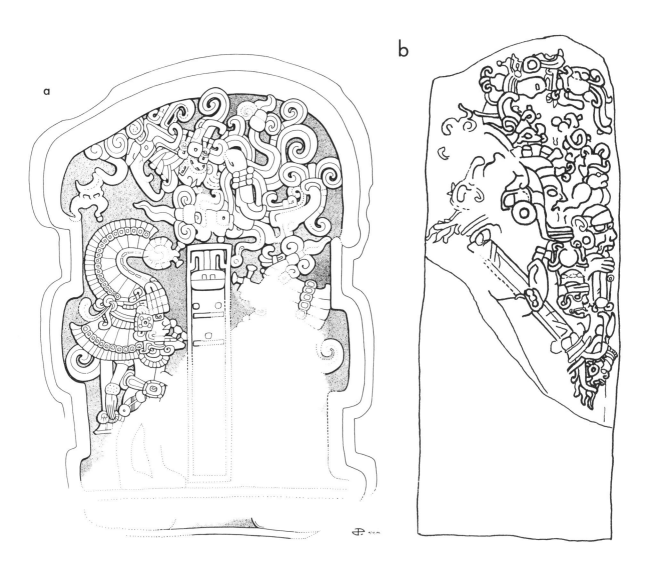

Fig. 45   Carvings from Abaj Takalik and Tikal. *a*. Stela 2, Abaj Takalik. Drawing by James Porter, courtesy of John Graham. *b*. Stela 29, Tikal (after W. R. Coe 1962: Fig. 5a).

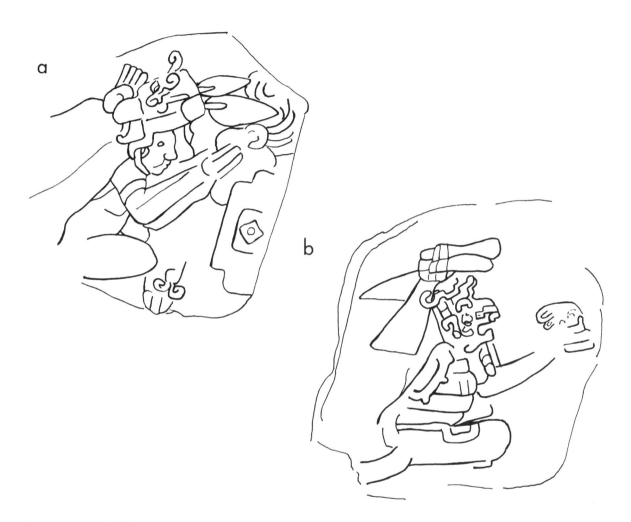

Fig. 46 Carved slabs from Dainzu. *a*. Seated figure (after Bernal 1968: 248). *b*. Seated jaguar or costumed figure (after Bernal 1968: 249).

a

b

Fig. 47 (*above*) Stela 3, La Venta (after Drucker et al. 1959: Fig. 67).

Fig. 48 (*right*) Altar 5, La Venta. *a*. South end. *b*. North end (after Stirling 1943: Plates 41a, b).

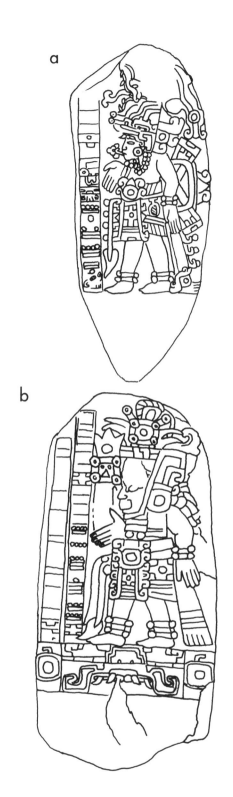

Fig. 49 (*left*)   Stelae 6 and 8, Cerro de las Mesas. *a*. Stela 6 (after Stirling 1943: Fig. 11b). *b*. Stela 8 (after Stirling 1943: Fig. 11c).

Fig. 50 (*above*)   Stela D, Tres Zapotes (after Stirling 1943; Fig. 4).

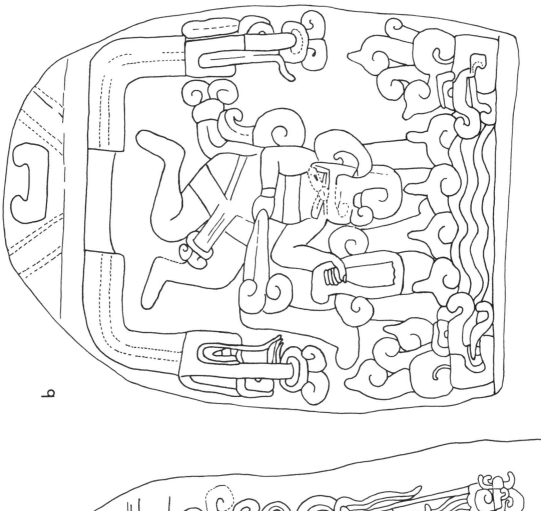

b

a

Fig. 51 Izapa Stelae Group 1. *a*. Stela 1. *b*. Stela 23.

a

b

Fig. 52 Izapa Stelae Group 2. *a.* Stela 6. *b.* Stela 26.

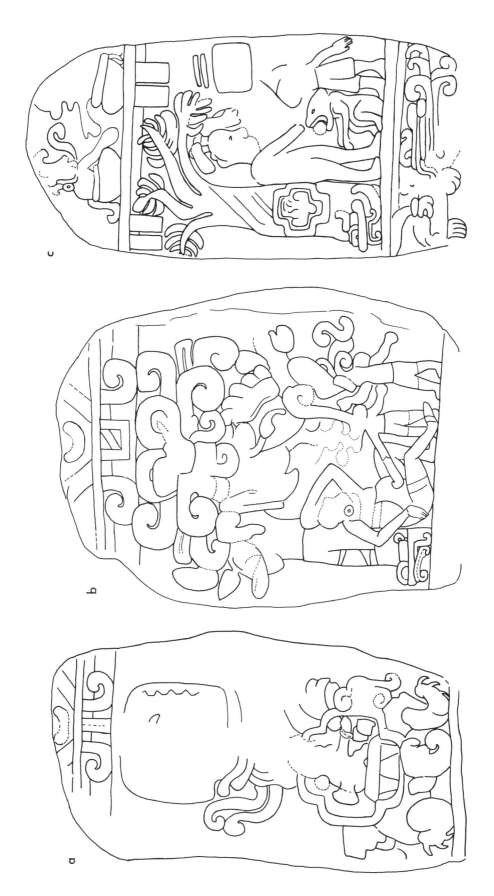

Fig. 53 Izapa Stelae Group 3. *a.* Stelae 8. *b.* Stela 10. *c.* Stela 27.

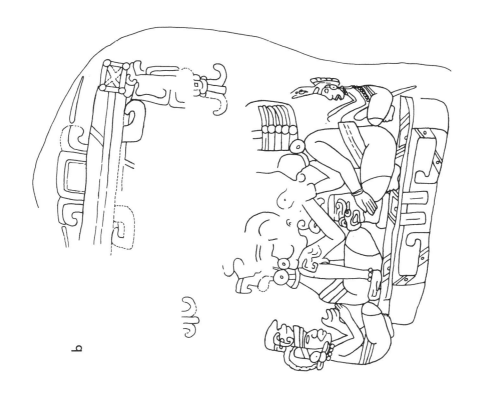

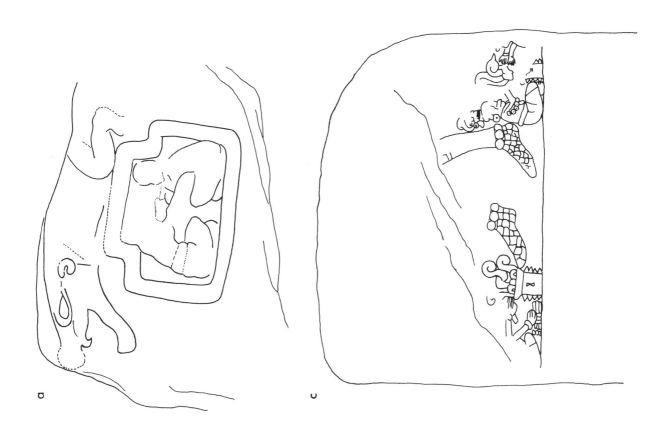

Fig. 54 Izapa Stelae Group 4. *a*. Stela 14. *b*. Stela 18. *c*. Stela 24.

a

c

b

d

e

g

f

Fig. 55   Izapa Stelae Group 5. *a*. Stela 2. *b*. Stela 4.
c. Stela 11. *d*. Stela 3. *e*. Stela 7. *f*. Stela 60. *g*. Stela 21.

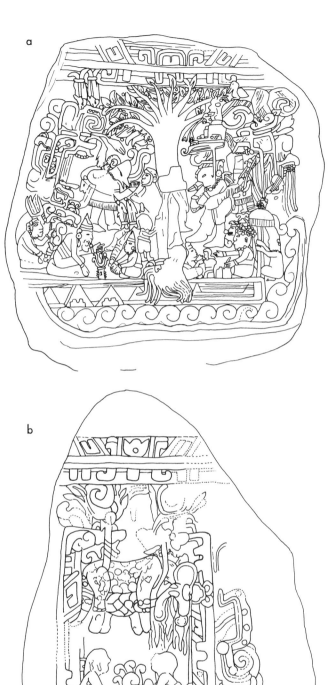

Fig. 56 Izapa Stelae Group 6. *a*. Stela 5. *b*. Stela 12. *c*. Stela 25.

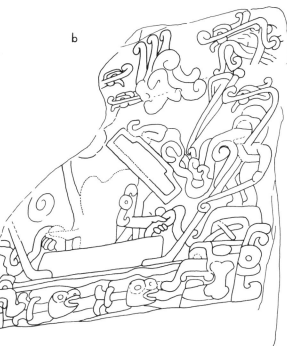

Fig. 57   Izapa Stelae Group 7. *a*. Stela 9. *b*. Stela 22.
c. Stela 67. *d*. Stela 50.

Bibliography

AGRINIER, PIERRE
  1960 *The Carved Human Femurs from Tomb 1, Chiapa de Corzo, Chiapas, Mexico.* Papers of the New World Archaeological Foundation 6, Orinda.

ARNHEIM, RUDOLF
  1954 *Art and Visual Perception.* University of California Press, Berkeley.

BADNER, MINO
  1972 *A Possible Focus of Andean Artistic Influence in Mesoamerica.* Studies in Pre-Columbian Art and Archaeology 9. Dumbarton Oaks, Washington.

BERGER, C. RAINER, JOHN A. GRAHAM, and ROBERT F. HEIZER
  1967 A Reconsideration of the Age of the La Venta Site. *Contributions of the University of California Archaeological Research Facility, Studies in Olmec Archaeology* 3: 1–24. Berkeley.

BERNAL, IGNACIO
  1968 The Ball Players of Dainzu. *Archaeology* 21 (4): 246–251.
  1969 *The Olmec World* (Doris Heyden and Fernando Horcasitas, trans.). University of California Press, Berkeley.

BOAS, FRANZ
  1955 *Primitive Art.* Dover Publications, New York.

CASO, ALFONSO
  1965a Sculpture and Mural Painting of Oaxaca. In *Handbook of Middle American Indians* (Robert Wauchope and Gordon R. Willey, eds.) 3: 849–870. University of Texas Press, Austin.
  1965b Zapotec Writing and Calendar. In *Handbook of Middle American Indians* (Robert Wauchope and Gordon R. Willey, eds.) 3: 931–947. University of Texas Press, Austin.
  1965c ¿Existio un imperio olmeca? *Memorias de El Colegio Nacional* 5 (3): 11–60. Mexico.

COE, MICHAEL D.
  1962 *Mexico.* Frederick A. Praeger, New York.
  1965 The Olmec Style and Its Distribution. In *Handbook of Middle American Indians* (Robert Wauchope and Gordon R. Willey, eds.) 3: 739–775. University of Texas Press, Austin.
  1968 *America's First Civilization.* American Heritage Publishing Co., in association with the Smithsonian Institution, New York.
  1972 Olmec Jaguars and Olmec Kings. In *The Cult of the Feline* (Elizabeth P. Benson, ed.): 1–18. Dumbarton Oaks, Washington.
  1973 *The Maya Scribe and His World.* The Grolier Club, New York.

  1976 Early Steps in the Evolution of Maya Writing. In *Origins of Religious Art and Iconography in Preclassic Mesoamerica* (H. B. Nicholson, ed.): 107–122. UCLA Latin American Studies Series 31. University of California at Los Angeles Latin American Center and Ethnic Arts Council of Los Angeles.

COE, MICHAEL D., and KENT V. FLANNERY
  1967 *Early Cultures and Human Ecology in South Coastal Guatemala.* Smithsonian Institution, Contributions to Anthropology 3. Washington.

COE, WILLIAM R.
  1962 A summary of Excavation Research at Tikal, Guatemala: 1956–61. *American Antiquity* 27 (4): 479–507.
  1967 *Tikal: A Handbook of the Ancient Maya Ruins.* University Museum, University of Pennsylvania, Philadelphia.

COVARRUBIAS, MIGUEL
  1946 El arte "Olmeca" o de La Venta. *Cuadernos Americanos* 5 (4); 153–179.
  1957 *Indian Art of Mexico and Central America.* Alfred A. Knopf, New York.

DILLEHAY, TOM D., and PETER KAULICKE
  n.d. Acercamiento metodologico: el comportamiento del jaquar y la organizacion socio-espacial humana. 1978. In *Actas Del V Congreso Nacional de Arqueología Argentina, San Juan, abril 1978,* Tomo 2. Universidad Nacional de San Juan. (In press.)

DRUCKER, PHILIP
  1948 Preliminary Notes on an Archaeological Survey of the Chiapas Coast. *Mid-American Research Records* 1 (11): 151–169. Tulane University, New Orleans.
  1952 *La Venta, Tabasco: A Study of Olmec Ceramics and Art.* Smithsonian Institution, Bureau of American Ethnology, Bulletin 153. Washington.
  1955 The Cerro de las Mesas Offering of Jade and Other Materials. *Smithsonian Institution, Bureau of American Ethnology, Bulletin* 157: 25–68. Washington.
  1981 On the Nature of Olmec Polity. In *The Olmec and Their Neighbors, Essays in Memory of Matthew W. Stirling* (Elizabeth P. Benson, ed.): 29–47. Dumbarton Oaks, Washington.

DRUCKER, PHILIP, ROBERT R. HEIZER, and ROBERT J. SQUIER
  1959 *Excavations at La Venta, Tabasco, 1955.* Smithsonian Institution, Bureau of American Ethnology, Bulletin 170. Washington.

EASBY, ELIZABETH KENNEDY, and JOHN F. SCOTT
1970 *Before Cortes: Sculpture of Middle America.* The Metropolitan Museum of Art. New York.

EKHOLM, SUSANNA M.
1969 *Mound 30a and the Early Preclassic Ceramic Sequence of Izapa, Chiapas, Mexico.* Papers of the New World Archaeological Foundation 25. Provo.

FISCHER, JOHN
1961 Art Styles as Cultural Cognitive Maps. *American Anthropologist* 63 (1): 79–93.

GRAHAM, JOHN A.
1977 Discoveries at Abaj Takalik, Guatemala. *Archaeology* 30 (3): 196–197.

GRAHAM, JOHN A., ROBERT F. HEIZER, and EDWIN M. SHOOK
1978 Abaj Takalik 1976: Exploratory Investigations. *Contributions of the University of California Archaeological Research Facility, Studies in Ancient Mesoamerica* 3: 85–109. Berkeley.

GUDGER, E. A.
1919 On the Use of the Sucking-Fish and Turtles: Studies in Echeneis and Remora. *The American Naturalist* 53: 289–311, 446–467, 515–525.

HATCHER, EVELYN PAYNE
1967 *Visual Metaphors: A Formal Analysis of Navajo Art.* West Publishing Co., New York.

HEATH-JONES
1959 Definition of an Ancestral Maya Civilization in Miraflores Phase: Kaminaljuyu. In *Abstracts of Papers, 24th Annual Meeting of the Society for American Archaeology* (D. A. Suhm, ed.): 37.

HOLM, BILL
1965 *Northwest Coast Indian Art.* University of Washington Press, Seattle.

JORDAN, DAVID STARR, and BARTON WARREN EVERMANN
1900 *The Fishes of North and Middle America: A Descriptive Catalogue of the Species of Fish-Like Vertebrates Found in the Waters of North America, North of the Isthmus of Panama.* United States National Museum Bulletin 47, Part 4. Washington.

KIDDER, ALFRED V., JESSE D. JENNINGS, and EDWIN M. SHOOK
1946 Excavations at Kaminaljuyu, Guatemala. *Carnegie Institution of Washington, Publication* 561. Washington.

KLEINBAUER, W. EUGENE
1971 *Modern Perspectives in Western Art History.* Holt, Rinehart, and Winston, New York.

KUBLER, GEORGE
1962 *The Shape of Time: Remarks on the History of Things.* Yale University Press, New Haven.
1967 *The Iconography of the Art of Teotihuacan.* Studies in Pre-Columbian Art and Archaeology 4. Dumbarton Oaks, Washington.
1969 *Studies in Classic Maya Iconography.* Memoirs of the Connecticut Academy of Arts and Sciences 18. New Haven.

LAMBERT, J. D. H., and J. T. ARNASON
1982 Ramon and Maya Ruins: An Ecological, Not an Economic, Relation. *Science* 216 (4543): 298–299.

LOTHROP, SAMUEL K.
1924 *Tulum, an Archaeological Study of the East Coast of Yucatan.* Carnegie Institution of Washington, Publication 335. Washington.

LOWE, GARETH W.
1965 Desarrollo y funcion del incensario en Izapa. *Estudios de Cultura Maya* 5: 53–64. Seminario de Cultura Maya. Universidad Nacional Autónoma de México, Mexico.

LOWE, GARETH W., and J. ALDEN MASON
1965 Archaeological Survey of the Chiapas Coast, Highlands, and Upper Grijalva Basin. In *Handbook of Middle American Indians* (Robert Wauchope and Gordon R. Willey, eds.) 2: 195–236. University of Texas Press, Austin.

MARCUS, JOYCE
1976 The Iconography of Militarism at Monte Alban and Neighboring Sites in the Valleys of Oaxaca. In *Origins of Religious Art and Iconography in Preclassic Mesoamerica* (H. B. Nicholson, ed.): 123–139. UCLA Latin American Studies Series 31. University of California at Los Angeles Latin American Center and Ethnic Arts Council of Los Angeles.

MILES, SUZANNE W.
1965 Sculpture of the Guatemala-Chiapas Highlands and Pacific Slopes, and Associated Hieroglyphs. In *Handbook of Middle American Indians* (Robert Wauchope and Gordon R. Willey, eds.) 2: 237–275. University of Texas Press, Austin.

MILLER, ARTHUR G.
1973 *The Mural Painting of Teotihuacan.* Dumbarton Oaks, Washington.

NORMAN, V. GARTH
1973 *Izapa Sculpture, Part 1: Album.* Papers of the New World Archaeological Foundation 30. Provo.
1976 *Izapa Sculpture, Part 2: Text.* Papers of the New World Archaeological Foundation 30. Provo.

PADDOCK, JOHN
1966 Oaxaca in Ancient Mesoamerica. In *Ancient Oaxaca* (John Paddock, ed.): 87–242. Stanford University Press, Stanford.

PANOFSKY, ERWIN
1939 *Studies in Iconology: Humanistic Themes in the Art of the Renaissance.* Harper Torchbooks, New York.
1960 *Renaissance and Renascences in Western Art.* Almquist and Wiksell, Stockholm.

PARSONS, LEE A.
1969   *Bilbao, Guatemala: An Archaeological Study of the Pacific Coast Cotzumalhuapa Region,* 2 vols. Publications in Anthropology 12. Milwaukee Public Museum, Milwaukee.

PERRY, RICHARD
1970   *The World of the Jaguar.* Taplinger Publishing Co., New York

PIRES-FERREIRA, JANE W.
1976a   Obsidian Exchange in Formative Mesoamerica. In *The Early Mesoamerican Village* (Kent V. Flannery, ed.): 292–306. Academic Press, New York.
1976b   Shell and Iron-Ore Mirror Exchange in Formative Mesoamerica, with Comments on Other Commodities. In *The Early Mesoamerican Village* (Kent V. Flannery, ed.): 311–328. Academic Press, New York.

PROSKOURIAKOFF, TATIANA
1950   *A Study of Classic Maya Sculpture.* Carnegie Institution of Washington, Publication 593. Washington.
1968   Olmec and Maya Art: Problems of Their Stylistic Relation. In *Dumbarton Oaks Conference on the Olmec, October 28th and 29th, 1967* (Elizabeth P. Benson, ed.): 119–134. Dumbarton Oaks, Washington.

PULESTON, DENNIS E.
n.d.   Brosimum Alicastrum as a Subsistence Alternative for the Classic Maya of the Central Southern Lowlands. MA thesis, University of Pennsylvania, Philadelphia, 1968.

PULESTON, DENNIS E., and OLGA STAVRAKIS PULESTON
1971   An Ecological Approach the the Origins of Maya Civilization. *Archaeology* 24 (4): 330–337.

QUIRARTE, JACINTO
1973   *Izapan-Style Art: A Study of Its Form and Meaning.* Studies in Pre-Columbian Art and Archaeology 10. Dumbarton Oaks, Washington.
1976   The Relationship of Izapan-Style Art to Olmec and Maya Art: A Review. In *Origins of Religious Art and Iconography in Preclassic Mesoamerica* (H. B. Nicholson, ed.): 73–86. UCLA Latin American Studies Series 31. University of California at Los Angeles Latin American Center and Ethnic Arts Council of Los Angeles.
1981   Tricephalic Units in Olmec, Izapan-Style, and Maya Art. In *The Olmec and Their Neighbors, Essays in Memory of Matthew W. Stirling* (Elizabeth P. Benson, ed.): 289–308. Dumbarton Oaks, Washington.

RAPPAPORT, ROY A.
1971   Ritual, Sanctity, and Cybernetics. *American Anthropologist* 73 (1): 59–76.

ROHLF, F. JAMES, JOHN KISHPAUGH, and DAVID KIRK
1974   *NT-SYS, Numerical Taxonomy System of Multivariate Statistical Programs.* The State University of New York at Stony Brook, Stony Brook.

SHELFORD, VICTOR E.
1963   *The Ecology of North America.* University of Illinois Press, Urbana.

SHOOK, EDWIN M.
1947   Guatemala Highlands. *Carnegie Institution of Washington, Year Book* 46: 179–184. Washington.

SOKAL, ROBERT R., and PETER H. A. SNEATH
1963   *Principles of Numerical Taxonomy.* W. H. Freeman and Co., San Francisco.

STIRLING, MATTHEW W.
1941   Expedition Unearths Buried Masterpieces of Carved Jade. *National Geographic Magazine* 80 (3): 278–302.
1943   *Stone Monuments of Southern Mexico.* Smithsonian Institution, Bureau of American Ethnology, Bulletin 138. Washington.

STOCKER, TERRY, SARAH MELTZOFF, and STEVE ARMSEY
1980   Crocodilians and Olmecs: Further Interpretations in Formative Period Iconography. *American Antiquity* 45 (4): 740–758.